Retro Quilts

15 Modern Designs with a Vintage Vibe

Maude MacDonald

DAVID & CHARLES
—PUBLISHING—

www.davidandcharles.com

Contents

Meet Maude — 6

Chapter 1: Quilting Essentials — 8

Tools & materials — 10
Assembling your quilt — 14
Drunkard's Path unit — 18
Half circle units — 21
Dresden plate units — 22
Appliqué — 24
Pillow backings — 26
Making a wall hanging — 28

Chapter 2: The Projects — 30

Beginner designs:
Chevy — 32
Static — 38
Good Vibes — 44
Stevie Pillow — 50

Confident beginner designs:
Patio Lanterns — 56
Outta Sight — 62
Flower Power — 68

Intermediate designs:
Checkered Adventure — 74
Op Art — 80
Appliqué Adventure — 86

Advanced designs:
Trippy Dippy — 94
Quilt 54 — 100
Light My Fire — 106
Retro Blooms — 114
High Fidelity — 122

Templates — 128
Glossary — 140
Index — 141
Acknowledgments — 143

Retro Quilts

Meet Maude

Hello, my quilty friend! I am so (SEW!) glad you're here. I'm Maude MacDonald, the Retro Quilter who, you guessed it, loves retro style and quilting.

I like to think that I didn't find quilting—rather that it found me, back in 2018. It was the holiday season and I needed a gift for my dad. I had the brilliant idea to make him a T-shirt quilt out of all his old NASCAR shirts. I mean, how hard could it be? Well, it turned out to be trickier than I thought, but Christmas morning he opened his gift and loved it. From then on, I was hooked, and constantly thinking about quilting, fabrics, and patterns. But what I wasn't seeing was my beloved retro style in quilt patterns, and so my journey into quilt pattern writing began.

Retro style for me isn't just something I like or integrate into my life here and there; it's my lifestyle. My home is retro, my clothes, cookbooks, and more. I've always been amazed by the sleek, cool styles of the 1960s and '70s, growing up in a house with hand-me-down teak furniture and stories from a hippie dad.

Even when I was a wee mini-Maude, I strove to be different and stand out, and retro style has always given me that edge. What I hope you get out of this book is a cool quilt that is totally you! The styles in this book are certainly retro, but they feel incredibly modern as well. What makes them unique is how YOU make them—the fabrics you pick, the finishing you choose—and I'm so honored you have chosen these patterns for that journey.

Keep creative and stay cool,

Maude

Quilting Essentials

Tools & materials

This section includes information on the tools and materials you will need to make the quilts in this book, as well as advice on fabrics, using the templates, and deciding which projects to make based on skill level.

Sewing machine
You need a basic sewing machine that doesn't give you trouble and makes a great consistent stitch. It is lovely to have the choice of additional stitches, especially for appliqué, like a satin, blanket, or zig zag stitch, but it's not necessary. It's a bonus if your machine has a ¼in (6mm) presser foot.

Presser foot
If your machine comes with a ¼in (6mm) presser foot, it is a great investment. I prefer one that has a partition to it so your fabric hits it and can't go past it into no man's land. If you don't have a presser foot, adding a strip of ¼in (6mm) tape to the base plate is a great alternative.

Thread
Aurifil 2026 in 50wt is my ride or die piecing thread. It aids in getting a nice flat seam, and because it's cotton, it will act the same as your cotton fabrics.

Rotary cutter
A 45mm is the go-to size for rotary cutters. Start a new quilt with a new blade for fewer headaches and more precise cutting. Smaller rotary cutters are great for smaller curves, but not necessary. I love my Olfa ergonomic rotary cutter.

Self-healing cutting mat
24 x 26in (60 x 66cm) is an ideal size, but you can absolutely make do with 18 x 24in (45 x 60cm). After trying many mats, my favorite is the Tattooed Quilter's version by Riley Blake.

Quilting rulers
My favorite is a 6.5 x 24in. A helpful ruler will be 4.5in square for a lot of the curved block patterns, and an 8.5in square for the Op Art pattern.

Iron and ironing board
Any iron will do, but I love my Oliso Smart Iron and my Oliso Mini. The mini is perfect for pressing seams, especially for blocks. Any ironing board will work as well.

Seam ripper
I know, but mistakes will happen, so let's be ready.

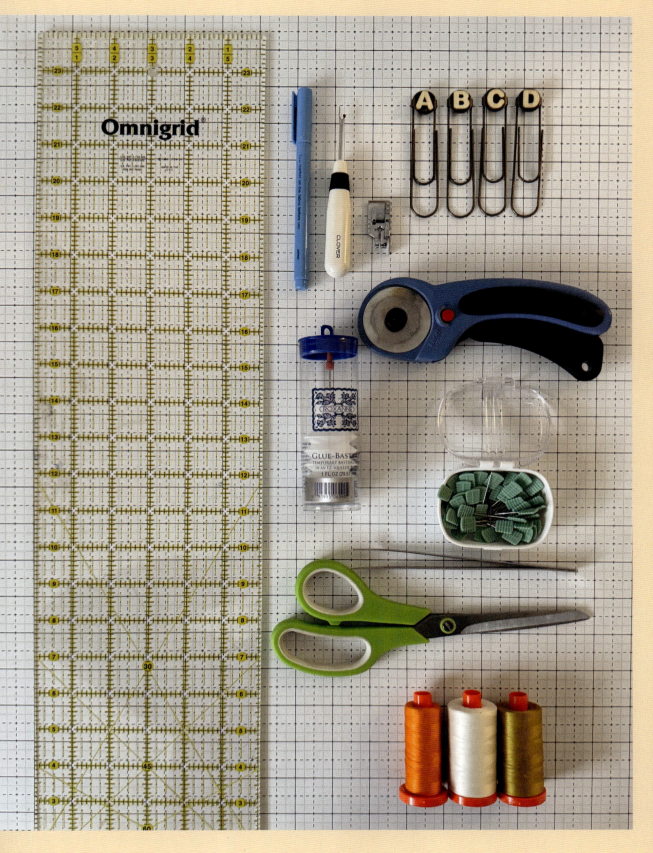

Glue

Look for a temporary glue that sets and holds well. My preferred glue is Roxanne Glue because it's sturdy, has a fine tip, sets fast with heat, and holds well. I use it all the time and it never disappoints.

Fusibles

Fusibles and interfacings are used for appliqué techniques. Appliqué paper is used for raw edge appliqué, while a fusible interfacing is great for turned appliqué. Both of these materials are widely available. A double sided fusible like Heat N' Bond appliqué paper is particularly great to work with.

Fabric scissors

You'll want fabric scissors to cut any appliqué out. Don't use paper scissors! Pinking shears are also good to use for appliqué.

Pins

Any straight pins of choice will work.

Starch

Some folks don't like starch—it's an extra step, and some starches can leave residue on fabric—but I love it. It's particularly useful when sewing curves because it helps to keep the fabric stiff, meaning it's less likely to warp. I like Magic Starch Spray, but you could also use a starch-free smoothing spray, such as Soak Flatter, if you prefer.

Sewing tweezers or stiletto

This helps with sewing curved blocks without glue or pins.

Templates

The templates you'll need to make the quilt projects are located at the back of the book. They have been included here at a reduced size (indicated by the percentage next to each template), and will need to be enlarged to full size and photocopied. If you don't have the facilities to do this at home, most good stationary stores will be able to do it for you for a small fee. Many of the templates can be reused in various projects throughout the book. Here are some suggestions to make your templates sturdier and last longer:

- Print and glue them to cardboard (a cereal box will do!).
- Acetate sheets can be traced and cut. Purchase these at quilt shops or dollar stores.
- Purchase acrylic templates from the Retro Quilter or Cut Once Quilts (where you can also purchase a 4½in (11.5cm) Drunkard's Path).

Water soluble marker

If you need to mark or trace on fabric, a water soluble marker is a great choice. Once you no longer need your markings, simply spray or dab some water onto the markings and they will disappear like magic! I have tried markers that "disappear" with the heat of an iron, and if these are for you, then do your thing! However, I've tested many of these and most markings seem to return when the fabric is cold, so a water soluble marker is my preferred option.

Fabric

Quilting cotton is the obvious choice when choosing fabric to make a quilt with. This is because there isn't any stretch and there is a ton of variety. It's durable, breathable, and cozy. You'll need fabric for the quilt top, backing, and binding for most projects in this book.

I used cotton fabrics from a variety of places to make the quilt projects in this book, including Ruby Star Society, Bella Solids by Moda Fabrics, Alice Apple Handmade, and Kona Solids. But this doesn't mean you can't sew with anything else! One of my favorite fabric picks will forever be vintage sheets, and I encourage you to experiment with different fabrics and suppliers as well. There are many types of fabric available, at different prices and offering different levels of warmth, so pick what's right for you.

Whatever sort of fabric you choose, my main advice would be to have contrast. If you were to do all low volumes, for example, the design would get lost. Take a photo of your fabric nominees and edit the photo into black and white for a clearer view on your contrast.

Labeling

To keep organized with constructing the patterns and for an easier sewing experience, it's important to label your pieces and units as each pattern instructs. And really, who doesn't want that? To do this there are a few options:

- Painter's (masking) tape and a marker
- Water soluble pen
- Labeling pins/clips

Skill levels

Each pattern in Retro Quilts has a suggested skill level: Beginner, Confident Beginner, Intermediate, or Advanced. The Beginner projects are for the brand-new quilter, while Intermediate is for the more seasoned quilter. Advanced is for quilters who are comfortable with their quilting skills and want a bit of a challenge. Please take these levels as suggestions—I encourage you to try patterns out and even learn some new skills!

Assembling your quilt

Here you will find all the information you need to assemble and finish your project. Quilting is quite the process, and I love every stage of it! Before we dive into all the fun of making these modern patterns with a retro flair, let's go over the stages of quilting.

1. Prep your fabric
The very first thing you should do after gathering your required fabrics together is press, starch, and cut them according to the pattern directions.

2. Piecing/Sewing
Follow the patterns in this book to assemble all that cut fabric back together again. You'll make a complete quilt top that will be a little larger than the finished size. Depending on the pattern, you can work block by block or chain-piece units to work into blocks later. Take your time and enjoy the process!

3. Create backing
For very large quilts you will need to join lengths of the backing material together to make the width of the quilt. Be aware of where the seams will fall—it might be better to have a full width of fabric in the middle with two equal-width smaller pieces on each side. If you need to join lengths of batting don't overlap the edges as this would make a bulky line—instead, lay the lengths with edges touching and machine sew together with the widest zig zag stitch on your sewing machine.

Creating backing from 42in (107cm) width fabric would be helpful—while smaller projects can get away with 1–2in (2.5–5cm) extra on each side, quilts need 4in (10cm) extra on each side. When lining up the seams, use vertical seams rather than horizontal if possible, so the quilting doesn't have to travel down the seam, just cross over it. You may also need to split a length of fabric so it's 21in (53.5cm) wide, sew end-to-end, then add to the 42in (107cm) wide strips to create your backing.

4. Basting
Assemble the layers with the backing wrong side up, then add the batting (wadding), then

the quilt top right side up on top of that. Basting (tacking) is the process of sandwiching the quilt top, the batting, and the backing all together temporarily. You can do this with basting pins, basting spray, or even Elmer's glue—choose whichever method suits you best. Always cut the batting and backing slightly larger than the quilt top to allow for the fabric that will be taken up by the quilt stitching. To minimize any slipping of the layers, start basting in the middle of the quilt and work out towards the edges.

5. Quilting

After basting all the quilt layers together, quilting is needed to permanently secure the layers together. For the projects in this book most of the quilting was done on a computerized longarm machine using a quilting pattern called a pantograph.

Alternatively, you can quilt your quilt at home on your domestic sewing machine. My favorite method is to use the seams of the quilt as a guideline and quilt straight lines. That way there's no marking needed—but if you want to do something more complex, go for it! My favorite marking tool is the Clover water soluble thick marker, but lots of folks use a Hera marker or painter's tape.

Sometimes though, I like to curl up on the couch with a work-in-progress quilt on my lap and hand stitch that baby. Hand quilting is a beautiful touch for any quilt. When I hand quilt, I use Aurifil 8wt thread or Aurifil Floss, which are thicker threads, to emphasize my stitches.

When it comes to quilting and choosing a method to use, I believe each quilt will have a different answer. Choose whichever one suits you best, or try something new! Any which way you quilt it, it's sure to be a beauty!

When you have finished, trim any excess batting and backing away even with the quilt top.

6. Binding

The last step in the quilting process is binding. This is where you seal

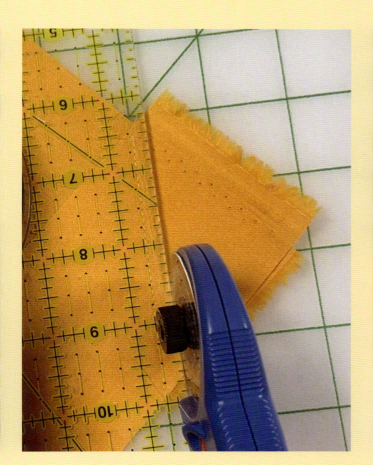

up the edges around the quilt. In this book, I've listed the fabric requirements for a 2½in (6.4cm) wide binding, which is what I prefer. But if that's not your jam, no worries! Make your binding by sewing all your fabric strips together and pressing it in half lengthwise. Open out the binding again and place it right sides together along one edge of your quilt—either on the front or back—aligning the raw edges and beginning in the middle of one side.

Fold over the beginning end by ½in (1.3cm). Sew the binding to the quilt along the first edge with a ½in (1.3cm) seam allowance until you are ½in (1.3cm) from the corner. Remove the quilt from the machine and fold the strip of binding at right angles, making a diagonal fold.

Hold the diagonal fold in place with a finger, then fold the binding down so it's aligned with the next raw edge of the quilt and continue sewing it down. Repeat this process at every corner. At the end, overlap the beginning of the binding and cut any excess binding away.

Fold the binding over the raw edges of the quilt, completely enclosing them. You will have a neat miter at each corner. Fold up the raw edge of the binding and sew in place either by machine or by hand. Binding can be made of either one fabric or many for a fun, scrappy look!

Other finishing ideas

I had the best time making the quilts in this book, and that extends to finishing the projects. I like to experiment with hand stitching, different trims, and edging. I also encourage you to step outside the box and try something different!

How about one of these?
- Rounded corners
- Ric Rac trim
- Fringe trim
- Hand stitched binding

Drunkard's Path unit

With this unit you need to sew a concave curve to a convex curve. For each of the construction methods, start by cutting your concave and convex pieces as accurately as possible, following the instructions in your pattern.

This technique is used in:
- Light My Fire
- Quilt 54
- Retro Blooms

Using pins for curves

1 Fold both concave (crust) and convex (pie) fabrics in half and fingerpress to crease the middle. Open the fabrics out and use this crease to align the pieces right sides together with the concave fabric on top.

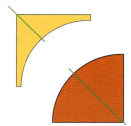

2 Pin the fabrics together, right sides together, at the middle crease with both edges aligned. Take one of the concave ends and swing it around so the flat end is aligned with the straight edge of the convex fabric. Pin in place. Repeat on the other side.

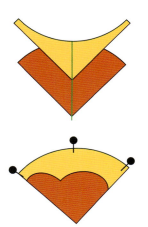

3 Now you have your middle and each end pinned, pin the edges together between these points, being careful not to stretch the fabrics. Don't worry about using too many pins!

4 Time to sew! Using your ¼in (6mm) presser foot and a smaller stitch length (1.8–2), start sewing at one end of the pinned fabric. As you sew, be mindful of keeping both fabrics aligned. Make sure the fabric under the needle is flat.

5 Once the seam is sewn you need to iron. Don't worry just yet if you have a little crease in your seam.

6 Use pinking shears to trim the seam allowance, if desired. Press the curved seam towards the concave piece.

7 That's it—you did it! Sewing curves takes some time and practice, but see—that wasn't so scary!

Using glue for curves

1 Repeat steps 2 and 3 of Using Pins for Curves on the previous page. Use a small bead of glue along the seam allowance instead of pins and set with an iron for step 3.

2 Repeat step 4 of Using Pins for Curves.

3 Starting at the middle, press the seam towards the concave fabric until you get to the end. Repeat on the other side.

Using nothing for curves

1 Start with the convex and concave pieces in the position shown, with right sides together. The tops of both pieces should be aligned.

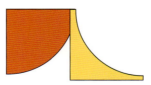

2 Align the top where the convex and concave pieces meet to the ¼in (6mm) indicator on your sewing machine. Start sewing slowly, aligning the curve of the concave piece to the curve of the convex piece.

3 Keep sewing slowly. You may need to stop, lift your presser foot and flatten the fabric, and that's OK. As long as the fabric under your needle is flat, you're good to sew.

4 Continue sewing until the ends meet. A pair of tweezers or a stiletto may be used to guide the ends through the machine.

5 Repeat steps 5–6 of Using Pins for Curves.

Trimming small Drunkard's Path units

NOTE
The large Drunkard's Path units in Retro Blooms will NOT be trimmed like this. Please see the instructions in the pattern for trimming.

1. Trim each Drunkard's Path to 4½ x 4½in (11.5 x 11.5cm) as follows: from the seam measure ¼in (6mm) towards the Template B fabric and trim. Repeat for the second Template B fabric edge, keeping the unit square.

2. Trim the remaining edges if necessary, using a quilter's square ruler to keep the edges at right angles.

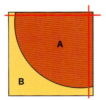

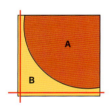

Hot tip
If you don't have the correct size ruler, simply mark the dimensions on the ruler you do have with painter's (masking) tape.

Half circle units

For this unit, start by cutting your concave and convex pieces as accurately as possible, following the instructions in your pattern.

> **This technique is used in:**
> - **High Fidelity**
> - **Trippy Dippy**

Using nothing for half circle curves

1. Start with the convex and concave pieces in the position shown, with right sides together. The tops of both pieces should be aligned.

2. Repeat all steps of Drunkard's Path Using Nothing for Curves.

Using pins for half circle curves

1. Gather the concave and convex pieces to make one block. Fold both pieces in half and fingerpress to crease the middle.

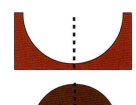

2. Open the fabrics out and use this crease to align the pieces right sides together with the concave fabric on top.

3. Start by pinning at the middle crease, then pin a bottom flat edge of the outer piece to the end of the straight edge of the inner piece. Repeat on the other side. Now the pieces are aligned, you can fill in between the joined points with more pins if you like.

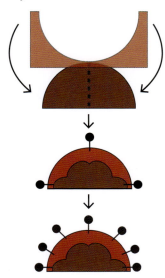

4. Sew the two curved edges together and press towards the concave piece. Trim seam allowance, if desired.

Dresden plate units

With this block you need to sew blades together to make a circle. The Dresden plates in this book have 20 blades. Start by cutting the blades you need following the instructions in your pattern.

This technique is used in:
- Op Art
- Stevie Pillow

Pointed blades

1 Fold a blade in half as shown and sew across the top folded edge. You can chain piece for faster sewing. To do this, sew one piece—without cutting the piece free—take a few more stitches, then sew the next piece. Continue until all the pieces are sewn, then cut them apart before pressing.

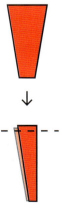

2 Snip across the corners as shown by the green lines, being careful not to cut through the stitching.

3 Flip the blade right side out, open the seam, and press.

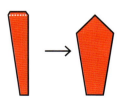

4 Place two blades with right sides together and sew, starting at the bottom of the blades and backstitching at each end.

5 Repeat step 4 until all the blades are sewn together in a circle. Press all the seams in the same direction.

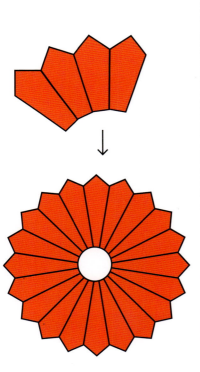

Wedge blades

1 Place a blade in the first color over a blade in the second color with right sides together. Beginning at the bottom of a blade, and backstitching top and bottom, sew the two pieces together as shown.

Hot tip
Sew the blades together in half- or quarter-circles before joining the full circle. It's a little easier to work with smaller units than adding blades to the whole, plus it makes your alignment more accurate.

2 Open out the blades and press the seam towards the darker fabric. Add the next blade in an alternate color in the same way. Repeat until you have a complete circle of blades in alternate colors, pressing all the seams in the same direction each time.

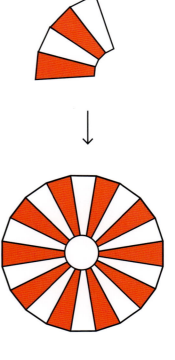

Appliqué

This is a method of creating designs by sewing fabric shapes on top of another fabric. It is often done using fun shapes and in layers. To make it easier, you can find templates at the back of the book for the appliqué motifs used here.

> **This technique is used in:**
> - Appliqué Adventure
> - Checkered Adventure
> - Flower Power
> - Op Art
> - Outta Sight

We'll be using fusible interfacing or a double-sided fusible webbing, such as Heat N' Bond appliqué paper, to fix the appliqué pieces in place.

Raw edge appliqué

1. Print, draw, or trace the designs from the templates section onto the paper side of the fusible appliqué paper. Remember the shape will be mirrored—you can reverse the image on the paper backing if necessary.

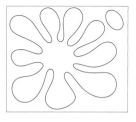

2. Cut out the designs roughly, leaving some space around them as shown.

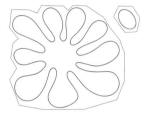

3. Place the fusible appliqué paper bumpy side (glue side) down and paper side up onto the wrong side of the desired fabric.

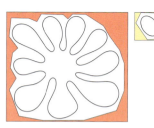

4. Press the fusible appliqué paper onto the fabric with an iron, following the manufacturer's instructions.

5. Allow to cool, then cut around the shapes on the paper side, through both fabric and fusible appliqué paper.

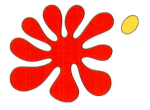

6. Carefully peel off the paper to reveal the adhesive layer.

7. Place the appliqué piece where desired and press into place with an iron, following the manufacturer's instructions.

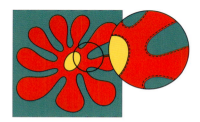

8. Finish the edges by sewing around the shape ⅛in (3mm) away from the edges. Zig zag or satin stiches could be used to enclose the raw edges more.

Turned edge fusible appliqué

1 Trace the designs from the templates onto the smooth side of the fusible interfacing.

2 Place the fusible interfacing glue side (bumpy) down onto the right side of the fabric piece.

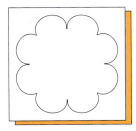

3 Sew all around on the outline drawn in step 1, backstitching at beginning and end.

4 Cut out the shape leaving a ¼in (6mm) seam allowance.

5 Snip into the seam allowance, close to but not through the seam, to allow the fabric to lie flat once it is turned right sides out. You could also use pinking shears to remove bulk.

6 Pull the layers of fabric and interfacing apart and make an approximately 2in (5cm) slit through the interfacing layer only. Use this slit to turn the shape right side out.

7 Smooth the edges and curves as much as possible, but DO NOT iron.

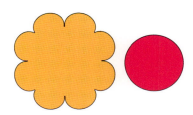

8 Place the appliqué shape on the backing fabric and press with an iron to fix in place, following the manufacturer's instructions.

9 Topstitch around the shape ⅛in (3mm) away from the edges.

Pillow backings

To make a pillow (once you have made the quilted top piece), you will need to add a backing to make the two layers to cover the pillow form.

> **This technique is used in:**
> - Appliqué Adventure
> - Flower Power
> - Outta Sight
> - Retro Blooms
> - Stevie Pillow

Envelope pillow back

1. You will have cut two pillow back rectangles in the cutting instructions for your project. On one of the longer edges, fold the fabric over to the wrong side twice by ½in (1.3cm) to make a double hem. Press in place and then topstitch along the inside fold. Repeat on the other pillow back piece.

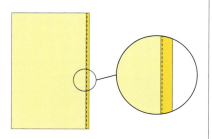

2. Lay the pillow front right side up. Place the first pillow back piece right side down with the hemmed edge at the center and all raw edges aligned.

3. Place the second pillow back piece right side down on the opposite side with the hemmed edge at the center and all raw edges aligned. The two pillow backs will overlap in the center by about 4in (10cm). Sew all around the edges with a ¼in (6mm) seam allowance.

4. Clip the corners—snip along the edges, in both directions, so the corner tip is only ⅛in (3mm) wide. This will reduce the bulk in the corner. Turn right side out through the opening in the back. Insert the pillow form and enjoy!

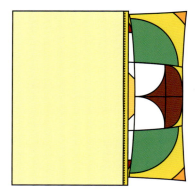

Round/shaped pillow back

1. Lay the quilted pillow top right side down on top of the pillow back fabric and pin in place.

2. Sew all around the edge with a ¼in (6mm) seam allowance, backstitching at beginning and end, and leaving a 4in (10cm) gap in one side.

3. Trim away any excess pillow back material. To make the seams flat, clip any curves or points.

4. Turn the pillow right side out through the gap in the seam. Gently smooth out any curves.

5. Insert the pillow form or stuff with polyester fiberfill then whipstitch the opening closed.

Pillow insert

1. Cut two pieces of plain fabric or calico (muslin) that are 1in (2.5cm) larger than the size needed for your pillow.

2. Lay the pieces right sides together, matching the raw edges. Sew all around the edge with a ¼in (6mm) seam allowance, backstitching at beginning and end, and leaving a 4in (10cm) gap in one side.

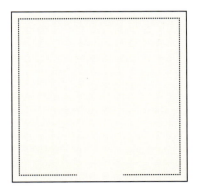

3. Clip across the corners and turn the insert right sides out through the gap in the seam. Stuff with polyester fiberfill then topstitch ⅛in (3mm) away from the edge to close opening, backstitching at the ends.

Making a wall hanging

Once you have finished your quilted wall hanging, use this simple method to add corners to the back of the wall hanging. This will allow you to attach a dowel rod to hang it with.

This technique is used in:
- Appliqué Adventure
- High Fidelity

1 Cut two 3½in (9cm) squares and fold each in half diagonally with wrong sides together to make triangles.

2 If you are binding your wall hanging, layer with batting and backing, quilt, and trim. Place the triangles on the back upper corners and baste in place using a ⅛in (3mm) seam. They will get sewn into the binding.

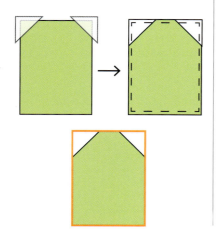

3 If your wall hanging is not being bound, quilt the piece with fusible fleece on the back. Lay the piece right side up. Lay the triangles on the right side upper corners and baste ⅛in (3mm) from edges.

Next, lay the backing right sides together on the quilted wall hanging and pin in place. Sew around the edges of the wall hanging using ¼in (6mm) seam allowance and leaving a 4in (10cm) gap. Backstitch at the beginning and end.

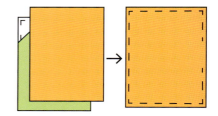

Clip corners and turn right sides out through the opening. Flip the triangle corners to the back Press, then top stitch around the entire project using a ⅛in (3mm) seam allowance, enclosing the opening.

 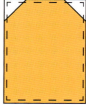

4 Insert the ends of a dowel rod into each triangle for hanging.

Chapter 2

The Projects

SKILL LEVEL
BEGINNER

Chevy

The muscle cars of the '60s and '70s made big statements, big sound, and big impact. With iconic hood ornaments and loud engines, they stood out and demanded attention. Incorporating the cool stripes of the '70s often found on the side of a sweet ride into the Chevy quilt creates the same impact now as those cars did then.

Tools & Materials

- Rotary cutter
- Cutting mat
- Fabric shears (optional)
- Pins
- Sewing machine
- Thread to match fabrics
- 6½ x 24in quilting ruler
- Metal straight edge
- Iron and ironing board

Fabric requirements

	Small	Medium	Large	Mega
Finished size	**48in (122cm) square**	**64in (162.6cm) square**	**80in (203.2cm) square**	**96in (243.8cm) square**
Fabric 1 (background)	1½ yards (137.2cm)	2 yards (182.9cm)	2¾ yards (251.5cm)	5⅝ yards (514.4cm)
Fabric 2 (chevron 1)	⅓ yard (30.5cm)	½ yard (46cm)	¾ yard (68.6cm)	⅞ yard (80cm)
Fabric 3 (chevron 2)	⅓ yard (30.5cm)	½ yard (46cm)	¾ yard (68.6cm)	⅞ yard (80cm)
Fabric 4 (chevron 3)	⅓ yard (30.5cm)	½ yard (46cm)	¾ yard (68.6cm)	⅞ yard (80cm)
Fabric 5 (chevron 4)	⅓ yard (30.5cm)	½ yard (46cm)	¾ yard (68.6cm)	⅞ yard (80cm)
Backing (with 4in/10cm overage)	3 yards (274.3cm)	4 yards (365.8cm)	6¼ yards (571.5cm)	8⅔ yards (792.5cm)
Batting/wadding (with 4in/10cm overage)	1½ yards, 60in wide (137cm, 152.4cm wide)	2 yards, 90in wide (182.9cm, 229cm wide)	2½ yards, 90in wide (229cm, 229cm wide)	3 yards, 120in wide (275cm, 304.8cm wide)
Binding (2½in/6.4cm strips)	½ yard (46cm)	⅝ yard (57.2m)	⅔ yard (61cm)	¾ yard (68.6cm)

Cutting

	Small	Medium	Large	Mega
Fabric 1	(2) 25½in (64.8cm) x WOF strips Subcut (2) 25½ x 30½in (64.8 x 77.5cm)	(2) 33½ (85cm) x WOF strips Subcut (2) 33½ x 39in (85 x 99cm)	(2) 48in (122cm) x WOF strips Subcut (2) 48 x 41½in (122 x 105.5cm)	(4) 49½in (125.8cm) x WOF strips Subcut (4) 49½ x 39in (125.8 x 99cm)
Fabric 2	(2) 5in (12.5cm) x WOF strips Subcut (2) 5 x 31½in (12.5 x 80cm)	(2) 6¾in (17.2cm) x WOF strips Subcut (2) 6¾ x 41in (17.2 x 104.2cm)	(3) 7¾in (19.7cm) x WOF strips Sew end to end Subcut (2) 7¾ x 50½in (19.7 x 128.3cm)	(3) 9½in (24.1cm) x WOF strips Sew end to end Subcut (2) 9½ x 60in (24.1 x 152.5cm)
Fabric 3	(2) 5in (12.5cm) x WOF strips Subcut (2) 5 x 31½in (12.5 x 80cm)	(2) 6¾in (17.2cm) x WOF strips Subcut (2) 6¾ x 41in (17.2 x 104.2cm)	(3) 7¾in (19.7cm) x WOF strips Sew end to end Subcut (2) 7¾ x 50½in (19.7 x 128.3cm)	(3) 9½in (24.1cm) x WOF strips Sew end to end Subcut (2) 9½ x 60in (24.1 x 152.5cm)
Fabric 4	(2) 5in (12.5cm) x WOF strips Subcut (2) 5 x 31½in (12.5 x 80cm)	(2) 6 ¾in (17.2cm) x WOF strips Subcut (2) 6¾ x 41in (17.2 x 104.2cm)	(3) 7¾in (19.7cm) x WOF strips Sew end to end Subcut (2) 7¾ x 50½in (19.7 x 128.25cm)	(3) 9½in (24.1cm) x WOF strips Sew end to end Subcut (2) 9½ x 60in (24.1 x 152.5cm)
Fabric 5	(2) 5in (12.5cm) x WOF strips Subcut (2) 5 x 31½in (12.5 x 80cm)	(2) 6 ¾in (17.2cm) x WOF strips Subcut (2) 6 ¾ x 41in (17.2 x 104.2cm)	(3) 7¾in (19.7cm) x WOF strips Sew end to end Subcut (2) 7¾ x 50 ½in (19.7 x 128.3cm)	(3) 9½in (24.1cm) x WOF strips Sew end to end Subcut (2) 9½ x 60in (24.1 x 152.5cm)
Binding	(6) 2½in (6.4cm) x WOF strips	(7) 2½in (6.4cm) x WOF strips	(9) 2½in (6.4cm) x WOF strips	(10) 2½in (6.4cm) x WOF strips

Note
- Please read through all the instructions before beginning.
- Fabric quantities assume a WOF of 42in (107cm).
- All seams have a ¼in (6mm) seam allowance.

Cutting instructions

1 On the two Fabric 1 rectangles for the size of quilt you are making, measure and mark the measurements shown in the diagram. Draw a line between the two marks to make trapezoids. You will need two pairs of trapezoids for your quilt. Note that for the **Mega** size you will start with four Fabric 1 rectangles and there will be two triangles that are not required (shown in gray on the illustration overleaf)—save them for another project.

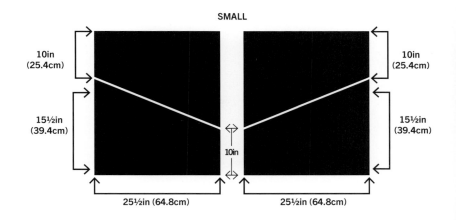

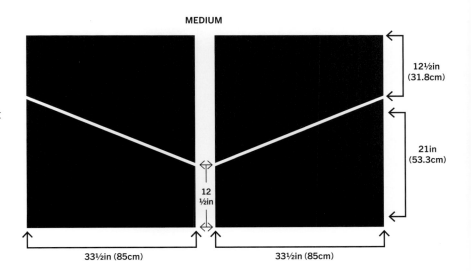

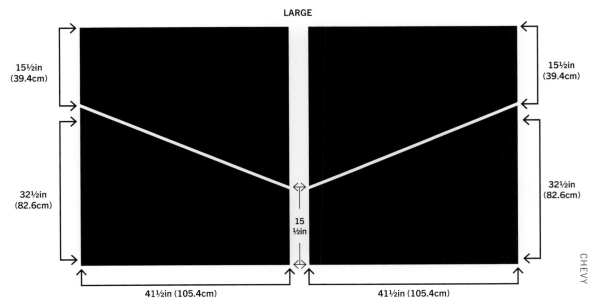

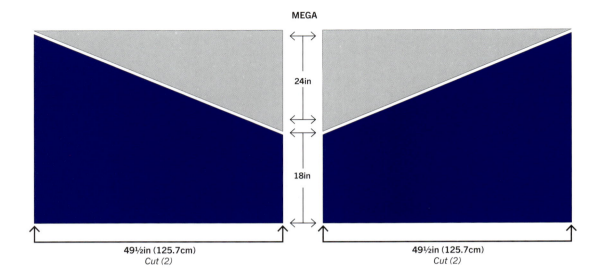

Quilt top construction

2. You will need two trapezoids in Fabric 1 (a lower and an upper one from one side for sizes **Small**, **Medium**, and **Large**, and two mirror image pairs for the **Mega** size) and one rectangle each of Fabrics 2, 3, 4, and 5. Start by placing one Fabric 2 rectangle right sides together on a trapezoid as shown in the diagram. The rectangle should overhang the trapezoid by no more than 1in (2.5cm) on the shorter side. Sew along the edge. Open out and press the seam towards the rectangle.

3. Now add Fabrics 3, 4, and 5 in the same way to create one half of the chevron.

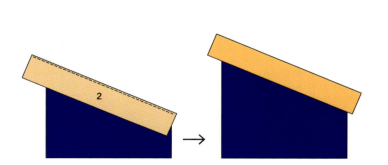

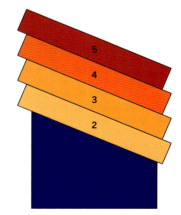

4 Using a long straight edge, trim the edges of the rectangles away so they are even with the edges of the trapezoid.

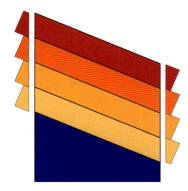

5 To add the matching trapezoid at the top, place it right sides down on the chevron matching the angled edge and offsetting the corners by ¼in (6mm). Sew along the edge then open out and press the seam towards the trapezoid. Trim the edges if they are not straight on each side. This completes one half of the quilt top.

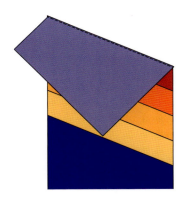

6 Repeat steps 2–5 to make the second half of the quilt top, this time pressing the seams towards the bottom each time.

7 Place the two halves with right sides together, matching all the seams down the middle. Don't worry if the top and bottom edges are not perfectly aligned as they can be trimmed later. Sew the seam, then open out and press the seam open.

8 Use the measurements below to trim the quilt top, which are from the center seam to the sides each time. Fold the quilt in half across the center and crease a fold line. Again use the measurements below from the fold to trim the top and bottom edges.

Small	24¼in (61.6cm)
Medium	32¼in (81.9cm)
Large	40¼in (102.2cm)
Mega	48¼in (122.6cm)

9 When the quilt top is complete, please refer to the "Assembling your quilt" section of the book and choose your preferred methods to layer, quilt, and finish your quilt.

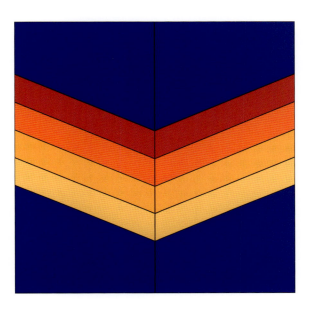

SKILL LEVEL
BEGINNER

Static

If you fell asleep on the couch with the television on in the days before Cable and 24-hour broadcasting, you'd most likely wake up to a static screen. With this static pattern quilt you can cuddle up with some nostalgia for those far out days!

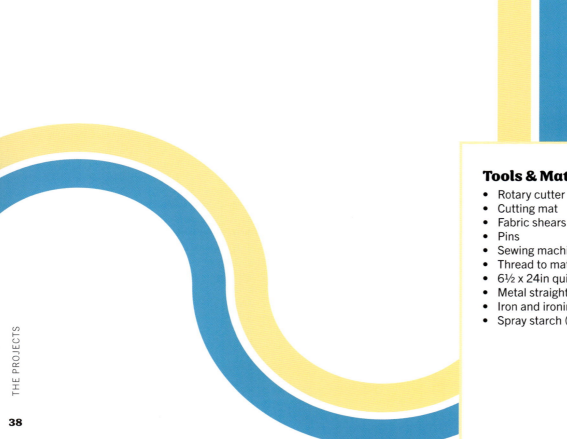

Tools & Materials

- Rotary cutter
- Cutting mat
- Fabric shears (optional)
- Pins
- Sewing machine
- Thread to match fabrics
- 6½ x 24in quilting ruler
- Metal straight edge
- Iron and ironing board
- Spray starch (optional)

Fabric requirements

	Small	Medium	Large	Mega
Finished size	42 x 45½in (107 x 115.5cm)	59½ x 67in (151 x 170.2cm)	70 x 82in (177.5 x 208.3cm)	84 x 101in (213.5 x 259cm)
Fabric 1 (white)	¼ yard (23cm)	⅝ yard (57.2cm)	⅝ yard (57.2cm)	1 yard (91.4cm)
Fabric 2 (yellow)	¼ yard (23cm)	⅝ yard (57.2cm)	⅝ yard (57.2cm)	¾ yard (68.6cm)
Fabric 3 (light blue)	¼ yard (23cm)	⅝ yard (57.2cm)	⅝ yard (57.2cm)	1 yard (91.4cm)
Fabric 4 (green)	¼ yard (23cm)	⅝ yard (57.2cm)	⅝ yard (57.2cm)	¾ yard (68.6cm)
Fabric 5 (pink)	¼ yard (23cm)	⅝ yard (57.2cm)	⅝ yard (57.2cm)	1 yard (91.4cm)
Fabric 6 (red)	¼ yard (23cm)	⅝ yard (57.2cm)	⅝ yard (57.2cm)	¾ yard (68.6cm)
Fabric 7 (dark blue)	¼ yard (23cm)	⅝ yard (57.2cm)	⅝ yard (57.2cm)	1 yard (91.4m)
Fabric 8 (black)	(1) Fat quarter OR ¼ yard (23cm)	½ yard (46cm)	⅝ yard (57.2cm)	¾ yard (68.6cm)
Fabric 9 (dark gray)	(1) Fat eighth OR ¼ yard (23cm)	(1) Fat eighth	(1) Fat quarter OR ⅓ yard (30.5cm)	(1) Fat quarter OR ⅜ yard (34.3cm)
Fabric 10 (medium gray)	(1) Fat eighth OR ¼ yard (23cm)	(1) Fat eighth	(1) Fat quarter OR ⅓ yard (31cm)	(1) Fat quarter OR ⅜ yard (34.3cm)
Fabric 11 (light gray)	(1) Fat quarter OR ⅓ yard (30.5cm) OR (1) 10 x 10in (25.4 x 25.4cm) square	(1) Fat eighth OR 13 x 7½in (33 x 19cm)	(1) Fat eighth	(1) Fat quarter OR ⅜ yard (34.3cm)
Backing (with 4in/10cm overage)	2 yards (183cm)	3⅞ yards (354cm)	5 yards (458cm)	9 yards (883cm)
Batting/wadding (with 4in/10cm overage)	1½ yards, 60in wide (137.2cm, 152.4cm wide)	2 yards, 90in wide (182.9cm, 228.6cm wide)	2¼ yards (205.7cm)	2⅝ yards, 120in wide (240cm, 304.8cm wide)
Binding (2½in/6.4cm strips)	⅜ yard (34.3cm)	½ yard (46cm)	⅝ yard (57.2cm)	¾ yard (68.6cm)

Hot tip

Try using textured tone-on-tone fabrics instead of solids to mimic the subtle static and scan lines of an old TV!

Note
- Please read through all the instructions before beginning.
- Fabric quantities assume a WOF of 42in (107cm).
- All seams have a ¼in (6mm) seam allowance.

Cutting instructions

1. Using a rotary cutter and cutting mat, cut all the pieces listed in the cutting table. Each piece has a letter label that identifies its size and color, to help with organization and construction later.

Cutting

	Small	Medium	Large	Mega	Piece label
Fabric 1	(1) 37½ x 6½in (95.3 x 16.5cm)	(1) 40½ x 9in (103 x 23cm)	(1) 40½ x 10½in (103 x 26.7cm)	(2) 40½ x 12½in (103 x 31.8cm)	A
		(1) 15½ x 9in (39.4 x 23cm)	(1) 25½ x 10½in (64.8 x 26.7cm)		A2
	(1) 3½ x 6½in (9 x 16.5cm)	(1) 5½ x 9in (14 x 9cm)	(1) 7½ x 10½in (19 x 26.7cm)	(1) 9½ x 12½in (24.1 x 31.8cm)	Z
Fabric 2	(1) 37½ x 6½in (95.3 x 16.5cm)	(1) 40½ x 9in (103 x 23cm)	(1) 40½ x 10½in (103 x 26.7cm)	(2) 40½ x 12½in (103 x 31.8cm)	B
		(1) 15½ x 9in (39.4 x 23cm)	(1) 25½ x 10½in (64.8 x 26.7cm)		B2
Fabric 3	(1) 37½ x 6½in (95.3 x 16.5cm)	(1) 40½ x 9in (103 x 23cm)	(1) 40½ x 10½in (103 x 26.7cm)	(2) 40½ x 12½in (103 x 31.8cm)	C
		(1) 15½ x 9in (39.4 x 23cm)	(1) 25½ x 10½in (64.8 x 26.7cm)		C2
	(1) 3½ x 6½in (9 x 16.5cm)	(1) 5½ x 9in (14 x 9cm)	(1) 7½ x 10½in (19 x 26.7cm)	(1) 9½ x 12½in (24.1 x 31.8cm)	Y
Fabric 4	(1) 37½ x 6½in (95.3 x 16.5cm)	(1) 40½ x 9in (103 x 23cm)	(1) 40½ x 10½in (103 x 26.7cm)	(2) 40½ x 12½in (103 x 31.8cm)	D
		(1) 15½ x 9in (39.4 x 23cm)	(1) 25½ x 10½in (64.8 x 26.7cm)		D2
Fabric 5	(1) 37½ x 6½in (95.3 x 16.5cm)	(1) 40½ x 9in (103 x 23cm)	(1) 40½ x 10½in (103 x 26.7cm)	(2) 40½ x 12½in (103 x 31.8cm)	E
		(1) 15½ x 9in (39.4 x 23cm)	(1) 25½ x 10½in (64.8 x 26.7cm)		E2
	(1) 3½ x 6½in (95.3 x 16.5cm)	(1) 5½ x 9in (14 x 9cm)	(1) 7½ x 10½in (19 x 26.7cm)	(1) 9½ x 12½in (24.1 x 31.8cm)	W
Fabric 6	(1) 37½ x 6½in (95.3 x 16.5cm)	(1) 40½ x 9in (103 x 23cm)	(1) 40½ x 10½in (103 x 26.7cm)	(2) 40½ x 12½in (103 x 31.8cm)	F
		(1) 15½ x 9in (39.4 x 23cm)	(1) 25½ x 10½in (64.8 x 26.7cm)		F2
Fabric 7	(1) 37½ x 6½in (95.3 x 16.5cm)	(1) 40½ x 9in (103 x 23cm)	(1) 40½ x 10½in (103 x 26.7cm)	(2) 40½ x 12½in (103 x 31.8cm)	G
		(1) 15½ x 9in (39.4 x 23cm)	(1) 25½ x 10½in (64.8 x 26.7cm)		G2
	(1) 3½ x 6½in (9 x 16.5cm)	(1) 5½ x 9in (14 x 9cm)	(1) 7½ x 10½in (19 x 26.7cm)	(1) 9½ x 12½in (24.1 x 31.8cm)	V
Fabric 8	(1) 10 x 6in (25.5 x 15.3cm)	(1) 10¾ x 7½in (27.3 x 19cm)	(1) 13¼ x 10½in (33.7 x 26.7cm)	(1) 15½ x 12½in (39.4 x 31.8cm)	H
	(1) 4½ x 6in (11.5 x 15.3cm)	(1) 9 x 7½in (23 x 19cm)	(1) 10½in (26.7cm) square	(1) 12½in (31.8cm) square	I
	(3) 3½ x 6½in (9 x 16.5cm)	(3) 5½ x 9in (14 x 23cm)	(3) 7½ x 10½in (19 x 26.7cm)	(3) 9½ x 12½in (24.1 x 31.8cm)	J
Fabric 9	(1) 7 x 6in (17.8 x 15.3cm)	(1) 10¼ x 7½in (26 x 19cm)	(1) 11¾ x 10½in (30 x 26.7cm)	(1) 14 x 12½in (35.5 x 31.8cm)	K
	(1) 2¾ x 6in (7 x 15.3cm)	(2) 3¾ x 7½in (9.5 x 19cm)	(1) 3¾ x 10½in (9.5 x 26.7cm)	(1) 4¾ x 12½in (12 x 31.8cm)	L
Fabric 10	(1) 7 x 6in (17.8 x 15.3cm)	(1) 10¼ x 7½in (26 x 19cm)	(1) 11¾ x 10½in (30 x 26.7cm)	(1) 14¼ x 12½in (36.2 x 31.8cm)	M
	(2) 2¾ x 6in (7 x 15.3cm)	(2) 3¼ x 7½in (8.3 x 19cm)	(2) 3¾ x 10½in (9.5 x 26.7cm)	(2) 4¼ x 12½in (10.8 x 31.8cm)	N
Fabric 11	(1) 9¼ x 6in (23.5 x 15.3cm)	(1) 13 x 7½in (33 x 19cm)	(1) 15½ x 10½in (39.4 x 26.7cm)	(1) 18½ x 12½ (47 x 31.8cm)	O
Binding	(4) 2½in (6.4cm) strips	(6) 2½in (6.4cm) strips	(8) 2½in (6.4cm) strips	(10) 2½in (6.4cm) strips	

Quilt construction

2 For the **Small** size only gather the A, B, C, D, E, F, and G pieces and lay them out in alphabetical order, then skip to step 3.

For the **Medium** and **Large** sizes gather the A, B, C, D, E, F, and G pieces and their corresponding A2, B2, C2, D2, E2, F2, and G2 pieces, as shown in the diagram to the right. Place the A2 piece right sides together and aligned with the top edge of the A piece. Sew the seam and press the seam in one direction. Repeat with all the other pairs, pressing the seam in alternate directions each time.

For the **Mega** size only sew the two A pieces together instead of an A and an A2, and repeat with the two B, C, D, E, F, and G pieces.

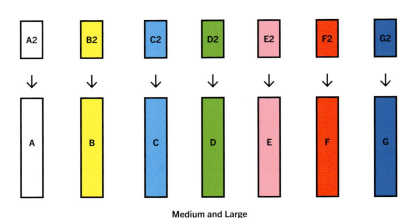

Medium and Large

3 For all sizes, gather all the V, J, W, Y, and Z pieces. Add each piece to the bottom end of the corresponding column as shown in the diagram to the right, pressing the seam in the same direction as the existing seam (if there is one) at the top of that column.

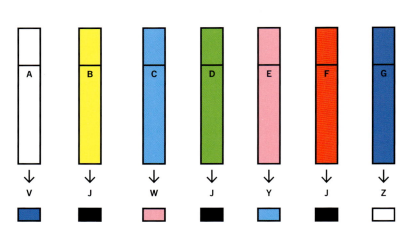

4 Place the first two columns right sides together, making sure to align all existing seams. Sew together from top to bottom, and then press the seam open. Add the other columns in order, changing the seam direction each time as indicated by the red arrows to avoid the piece bowing.

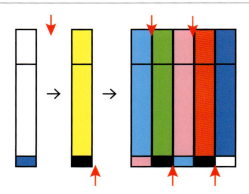

5 Gather all the H, K, M, O, N, L, and I pieces. Arrange them in the order shown, then sew them together in a row and press all the seams open.

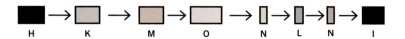

6 Sew this last row onto the bottom of the quilt top, matching all seams. Press this seam open.

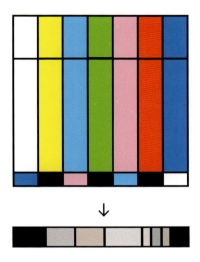

7 When the quilt top is complete, refer to the "Assembling your quilt" section and choose your preferred methods to layer, quilt, and finish your quilt.

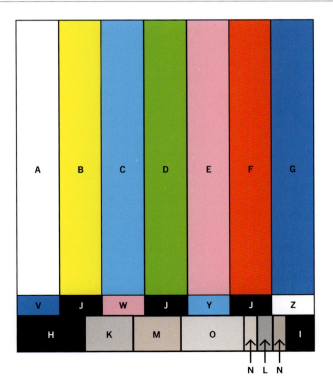

SKILL LEVEL
BEGINNER

Good Vibes

This is a fun and easy quilt inspired by the crocheted granny square Afghans of the 1970s. I used scraps from all the other quilts in the book to make it, but you could experiment with up to 100 different fabrics! This simple pattern offers maximum nostalgia vibes and is perfect for 2½in (6.4cm) strips.

Tools & Materials

- Rotary cutter
- Cutting mat
- Fabric shears (optional)
- Pins
- Sewing machine
- Thread to match fabrics
- 6½ x 24in quilting ruler
- Metal straight edge
- Iron and ironing board
- Spray starch (optional)

Fabric requirements

	Small	Medium	Large	Mega
Finished size	50 x 62in (127 x 157.5cm) 5 rows of 4 blocks	62 x 74in (157.5 x 188cm) 6 rows of 5 blocks	74 x 86in (188 x 218.5cm) 7 rows of 6 blocks	98 x 110in (249 x 279.5cm) 8 rows of 9 blocks
Prints/solids	(10) ¼ yard (23cm) cuts OR (30) various 2½in (6.4cm) precut strips	(10) ⅜ yard (34.3cm) cuts OR (45) various 2½in (6.4cm) precut strips	(10) ⅝ yard (57.2cm) cuts OR (63) various 2½in (6.4cm) precut strips	(10) ⅞ yard (80cm) cuts OR (108) various 2½in (6.4cm) precut strips
Black sashing	1¼ yards (114.3cm)	1½ yards (137.2cm)	2⅛ yards (194.3cm)	3⅓ yards (304.8cm)
Backing (with 4in/10cm overage)	3¼ yards (297.2cm)	3½ yards (320cm)	5¼ yards (480cm)	9⅞ yards (903cm)
Batting/wadding (with 4in/10cm overage)	2 yards (182.9cm)	2 yards (182.9cm)	2⅝ yards (240cm)	3 yards, 120in wide (274.3cm, 304.8cm wide)
Binding (2½in/6.4cm strips)	½ yard (46cm)	⅝ yard (57.2cm)	⅔ yard (61cm)	⅞ yard (80cm)

Cutting

	Small	Medium	Large	Mega	Piece label
Finished size	5 rows of 4 blocks	6 rows of 5 blocks	7 rows of 6 blocks	8 rows of 9 blocks	
Prints/solids	(30) 2½in (6.4cm) x WOF of various fabrics	(45) 2½in (6.4cm) x WOF of various fabrics	(63) 2½in (6.4cm) x WOF of various fabrics	(108) 2½in (6.4cm) x WOF of various fabrics	
	From (10) strips	From (15) strips	From (21) strips	From (36) strips	
	Subcut (2) 2½in (6.4cm) squares	Subcut (2) 2½in (6.4cm) squares	Subcut (2) 2½in (6.4cm) squares	Subcut (2) 2½in (6.4cm) squares	A
	Subcut (4) 2½in (6.4cm) squares	Subcut (4) 2½in (6.4cm) squares	Subcut (4) 2½in (6.4cm) squares	Subcut (4) 2½in (6.4cm) squares	B
	Subcut (4) 2½ x 6½in (6.4 x 16.5cm)	Subcut (4) 2½ x 6½in (6.4 x 16.5cm)	Subcut (4) 2½ x 6½in (6.4 x 16.5cm)	Subcut (4) 2½ x 6½in (6.4 x 16.5cm)	C
	From (20) strips	From (30) strips	From (42) strips	From (72) strips	
	Subcut (2) 2½ x 6½in (6.4 x 16.5cm)	Subcut (2) 2½ x 6½in (6.4 x 16.5cm)	Subcut (2) 2½ x 6½in (6.4 x 16.5cm)	Subcut (2) 2½ x 6½in (6.4 x 16.5cm)	D
	Subcut (2) 2½ x 10½in (6.4 x 26.7cm)	Subcut (2) 2½ x 10½in (6.4 x 26.7cm)	Subcut (2) 2½ x 10½in (6.4 x 26.7cm)	Subcut (2) 2½ x 10½in (6.4 x 26.7cm)	E
Black sashing	(15) 2½in (6.4cm) x WOF strips	(20) 2½in (6.4cm) x WOF strips	(28) 2½in (6.4cm) x WOF strips	(45) 2½in (6.4cm) x WOF strips	
	From (7) strips	From (9) strips	From (13) strips	From (21) strips	
	Subcut (25) 2½ x 10½in (6.4 x 26.7cm)	Subcut (36) 2½ x 10½in (6.4 x 26.7cm)	Subcut (49) 2½ x 10½in (6.4 x 26.7cm)	Subcut (81) 2½ x 10½in (6.4 x 26.7cm)	F
	Set aside (8) strips for sashing	Set aside (11) strips for sashing	Set aside (15) strips for sashing	Set aside (24) strips for sashing	G
Binding	(6) 2½in (6.4cm) x WOF strips	(8) 2½in (6.4cm) x WOF strips	(9) 2½in (6.4cm) x WOF strips	(11) 2½in (6.4cm) x WOF strips	

Note

- Please read through all the instructions before beginning.
- Fabric quantities assume a WOF of 42in (107cm).
- All seams have a ¼in (6mm) seam allowance.

Cutting instructions

1. Following the cutting table, cut as many 2½in (6.4cm) wide pieces from each fabric as you need for the size you are making. Each piece has a letter label that will help with organization and construction later. If you are using a jelly roll, this is already in 2½in (6.4cm) wide x WOF strips.

To get the concentric squares effect, pieces B and C should be the same color or print, and pieces D and E should also be the same. The diagram below shows what pieces you will need for one block.

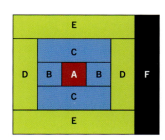

Block construction

2. Begin with A as the center. Place one B piece right sides together on A and sew the right-hand side seam. Repeat with another piece B on the left and then press the seams open.

3. Place one C piece with right sides together on top of the section already assembled, aligning the top edge seam. Sew the seam. Repeat to add a second C piece along the bottom edge and then press the seams open.

4. Place one D piece right sides together on top of the piece, aligning the right-hand edge, and then sew the seam. Repeat to add a second D piece on the left-hand edge as shown below. Press both seams open.

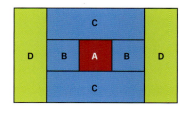

5. Next, place one piece E with right sides together on top of the section already assembled, aligning the top edge seam. Sew the seam. Repeat to add a second piece E along the bottom edge, then press the seams open.

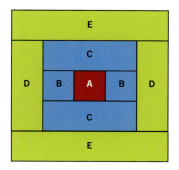

6. Place one piece F right sides together on top of the piece, aligning the right-hand edge and then sew the seam. Press the seam open. The finished block should measure 10½ x 12½ in (26.7 x 31.8cm).

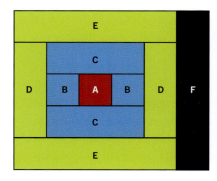

7. Repeat steps 2–6 to make as many blocks as you need for the size of quilt you are making:

    Small 20 blocks
  Medium 30 blocks
    Large 42 blocks
    Mega 72 blocks

Quilt construction

8 Lay out the blocks in rows to the size you are making and move them around until you are happy with the arrangement. Place one piece F right sides together on top of the piece, aligning it with the left-hand edge of the first block on the left. Sew the seam and press it open. Then add blocks on the right-hand side in order, to make up the first row.

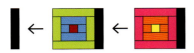

9 Repeat until all the rows are complete for the size of quilt you are making:

Small	5 rows of 4 blocks
Medium	6 rows of 5 blocks
Large	7 rows of 6 blocks
Mega	9 rows of 8 blocks

10 Sew the G strips end to end to make one long strip. Press the seams open. Cut the following sashing strips:

Small	(6) 2½ x 50½ in (6.4 x 128.3cm)
Medium	(7) 2½ x 62½ in (6.4 x 158.8cm)
Large	(8) 2½ x 74½ in (6.4 x 189.3cm)
Mega	(10) 2½ x 98½ in (6.4 x 250.3cm)

11 Place the first sashing strip right sides together on top of the top row, aligned with the top edge, as shown in the diagram at the bottom of the page. Sew the seam and press it open.

12 Sew a sashing strip to the top edge of each row and then sew the rows together.

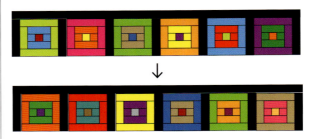

13 When all the rows are sewn together, sew the last sashing strip along the bottom edge of the quilt.

14 When the quilt top is complete, refer to "Assembling your quilt" and choose your preferred methods to layer, quilt, and finish your quilt.

Hot tip

You can make this quilt as scrappy as you like; it's a fabulous stash-busting opportunity!

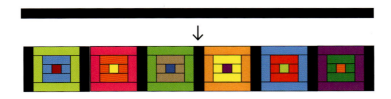

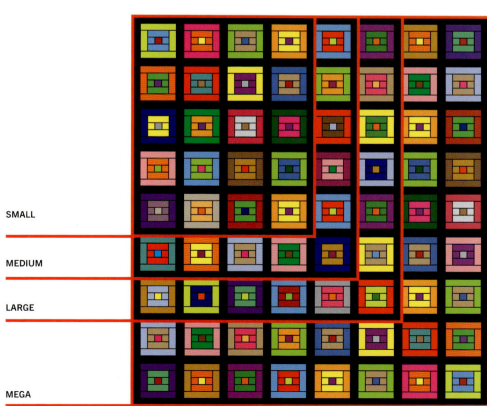

SMALL

MEDIUM

LARGE

MEGA

**SKILL LEVEL
BEGINNER**

Stevie Pillow

This design is inspired by the Bargello crocheted pillows of the 1970s, which made their way into the '80s and my childhood. While it looks complicated, the construction is easy enough for a beginner and will give a fun, retro vibe to any space.

Tools & Materials

- Rotary cutter
- Cutting mat
- Stevie Pillow templates
- Fabric shears (optional)
- Pins
- Fabric glue (optional)
- Sewing machine
- Thread to match fabrics
- Pinking shears (optional)
- Stiletto or tweezers
- 6½ x 24in quilting ruler
- Metal straight edge
- Iron and ironing board
- Pillow pad to match size you are making

Fabric requirements

	Small Pillow	Medium Pillow	Large Pillow	Mega Pillow
Finished size	14¾in (37.5cm) diameter	17¼in (44cm) diameter	20¼in (51.5cm) diameter	23¾in (60.5cm) diameter
Fabric 1 (center circle and first ring)	(1) Fat quarter	(1) Fat quarter	(1) Fat quarter	(1) Fat quarter
Fabric 2 (second ring from center)		(1) Fat quarter	(1) Fat quarter	(1) Fat quarter
Fabric 3 (third ring from center)			(1) Fat quarter	(1) Fat quarter
Fabric 4 (outer ring)				(1) Fat quarter
Lightweight fusible interfacing	⅛ yard (11.4cm)	⅛ yard (11.4cm)	⅛ yard (11.4cm)	⅛ yard (11.4cm)
Background/pillow back	½ yard (45.7cm)	⅝ yard (57.2cm)	⅝ yard (57.2cm)	1 ½ yards (137.1cm)
Backing (with 1in/10cm overage)	½ yard (45.7cm)	⅝ yard (57.2cm)	⅔ yard (61cm)	¾ yard (68.6cm)
Batting/wadding (with 4in/10cm overage)	(1) 16¾in (42.5cm) square	(1) 19¼in (48.9cm) square	(1) 22¼in (56.5cm) square	(1) 25¾in (65.4cm) square

Cutting

	Small Pillow	Medium Pillow	Large Pillow	Mega Pillow	Piece label
Fabric 1	(2) 5in (12.5cm) x WOFQ strips	(2) 5in (12.5cm) x WOFQ strips	(2) 5in (12.5cm) x WOFQ strips	(2) 5in (12.5cm) x WOFQ strips	
	Subcut (20) Small Dresden Blade templates	Subcut (20) Small Dresden Blade templates	Subcut (20) Small Dresden Blade templates	Subcut (20) Small Dresden Blade templates	A
Fabric 2		(3) 4in (10.2cm) x WOFQ strips	(3) 4in (10.2cm) x WOFQ strips	(3) 4in (10.2cm) x WOFQ strips	
		Subcut (20) Medium Dresden Blade templates	Subcut (20) Medium Dresden Blade templates	Subcut (20) Medium Dresden Blade templates	B
Fabric 3			(3) 4in (10.2cm) x WOFQ strips	(3) 4in (10.2cm) x WOFQ strips	
			Subcut (20) Large Dresden Blade templates	Subcut (20) Large Dresden Blade templates	C
Fabric 4				(4) 4in (10.2cm) x WOFQ strips	
				Subcut (20) Mega Dresden Blade templates	D
Lightweight fusible interfacing	4in (10.2cm) square	4in (10.2cm) square	4in (10.2cm) square	4in (10.2cm) square	
Background and pillow back	(1) 15¾in (40cm) x WOF strip	(1) 18¼in (46.4cm) x WOF strip	(1) 21¼in (54cm) x WOF strip	(2) 24¾in (62.9cm) x WOF strips	
	Subcut (2) 15¾in (40cm) squares	Subcut (2) 18¼in (46.4cm) squares	Subcut (2) 21¼in (54cm) squares	Subcut (2) 24¾in (62.9cm) squares	
Backing (with 1in/10cm overage)	(1) 16¾in (42.5cm) x WOF strip	(1) 19¼in (48.9cm) x WOF strip	(1) 22¼in (56.5cm) x WOF strip	(1) 25¾in (65.4cm) x WOF strips	
	Subcut (2) 16¾in (42.5cm) squares	Subcut (2) 19¼in (50.2cm) squares	Subcut (2) 22¼in (56.5cm) squares	Subcut (2) 25¾in (65.4cm) squares	
Batting/wadding (with 1in/10cm overage)	(1) 16¾in (42.5cm) square	(1) 19¼in (48.9cm) square	(1) 22¼in (56.5cm) square	(1) 25¾in (65.4cm) square	

Note

- Please read through all the instructions before beginning.
- Fabric quantities assume a WOF of 42in (107cm).
- An 18 degree Dresden ruler could be used in place of the Dresden blade templates.
- All seams have a ¼in (6mm) seam allowance.

Hot tip

If you are using an 18 degree Dresden ruler instead of the templates, the measurements are: Small 0–5in, Medium 2–6in, Large 3–7in, Mega 4–8in.

Cutting instructions

1. Using a rotary cutter and cutting mat, cut WOFQ strips as given in the cutting list. All the cut pieces have a letter label in the cutting list, which will help with organization and construction later. Subcut the strips into the relevant size Dresden Plate blades by rotating the template by 180 degrees after each cut.

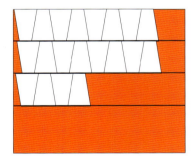

2. Copy and cut out the quarter-circle template for the size you are making. For the pillow appliqué background, fold one of the background/pillow back squares in half in both directions and place the quarter-circle template on top, aligned with the folded edges. Trim the fabric to the template, creating a circle. Label this as piece E.

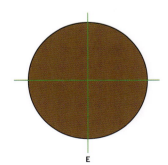

3. Cut a 4in (10cm) square from any fabric for the center circle and label this piece as F.

Dresden plate construction

Follow steps 4–6 and add the following pieces to piece E: For the **Small** size, add A pieces, then move to step 8. For the **Medium** size, add B then A pieces in that order. For the **Large** size add pieces C, B, and A in that order. For the **Mega** size add pieces D, C, B, and A in that order.

4. Gather all the blades needed for the size you are making and follow the Dresden Plate Pointed Blade instructions in the Quilting Essentials chapter.

5 Fold piece E in half in both directions and fingerpress to mark the center. Lay right side up and then lay the outermost Dresden Plate right side up on top, aligning the seams at the creases as shown below.

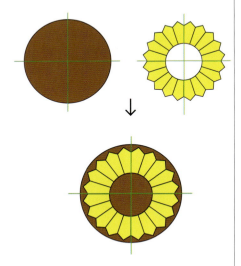

6 Pin or glue to hold in place and then topstitch along the pointed edges all around with an ⅛in (3mm) seam allowance.

7 Continue adding Dresden Plates in the correct order for the size you are making. Press each plate flat.

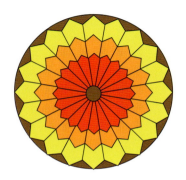

Dresden plate center

8 Use the Dresden Center circle template to trace a Dresden Center circle on the smooth side of the fusible interfacing square.

9 Using the F square and fusible interfacing square, follow steps 2–7 of Turned Edge Fusible Appliqué in the Quilting Essentials chapter.

10 Fold the circle in half in both directions to find the center and fingerpress to crease (do not iron yet). Place the center circle right side up over the hole in center of the Dresden Plate, aligning the creases with seams on the Dresden Plate. Once you are happy with the position, use a hot iron to fuse the center circle to the Dresden Plate following the manufacturer's instructions for the fusible interfacing.

11 Top stitch around the circle, ⅛in (3mm) from the edge.

Pillow construction

12 When the pillow top is complete, use your preferred methods to layer, quilt, and finish your pillow top.

13 Follow the Round/Shaped Pillow Back instructions in the Quilting Essentials chapter to fill and add the back for your pillow.

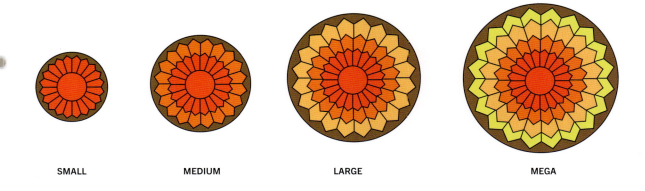

SMALL MEDIUM LARGE MEGA

**SKILL LEVEL
CONFIDENT BEGINNER**

Patio Lanterns

Who's ready for a party? I know I'm always up for a retro party! Patio Lanterns is inspired by party lights, and amazing lighting fixtures that are still so modern today. This pattern is fat quarter friendly and it would be fun to feature cool prints for the lantern fabrics.

Hot tip
Directional print fabric is not recommended for this pattern.

Tools & Materials
- Rotary cutter
- Cutting mat
- Triangle template (see Templates)
- Lanterns template (see Templates)
- 6½ x 24in quilting ruler
- Metal straight edge
- Fabric shears (optional)
- Pins
- Sewing machine
- Thread to match fabrics
- Iron and ironing board

Fabric requirements

	Small	Medium	Large	Mega
Finished size	45 x 50½in (114.3 x 128.3cm)	60 x 65in (152.5 x 165cm)	75 x 79½in (195.5 x 202cm)	90 x 94in (228.5 x 238.8cm)
Fabric 1 (lanterns)	4 fat quarters	6 fat quarters	10 fat quarters	13 fat quarters
Fabric 2 (joining rods)	⅛ yard (11.4cm)	⅛ yard (11.4cm)	¼ yard (22.9cm)	¼ yard (22.9cm)
Fabric 3 (background)	1¾ yards (160cm)	2¾ yards (251.2cm)	4 yards (365.8cm)	5½ yards (503cm)
Backing (with 4in/10cm overage)	2¼ yards (205.7cm)	4⅛ yards (377.2cm)	5⅝ yards (514.4cm)	8½ yards (777.2cm)
Batting/wadding (with 4in/10cm overage)	1⅝ yards, 60in wide (148.6cm, 152.4cm wide)	2 yards (182.9cm)	2½ yards (228.6cm)	2⅞ yards, 120in wide (262.9cm, 304.8cm wide)
Binding (2½in/6.4cm strips)	½ yard (45.7cm)	⅝ yard (57.2cm)	⅔ yard (61cm)	¾ yard (68.6cm)

Cutting

	Small	Medium	Large	Mega	Piece label
Fabric 1	Per fat quarter: (3) 6½in (16.5cm) x LOFQ Subcut (4) lantern templates per strip Total lantern pieces needed: 42	Per fat quarter: (3) 6½ in (16.5cm) x LOFQ Subcut (4) lantern templates per strip Total lantern pieces needed: 72	Per fat quarter: (3) 6½ in (16.5cm) x LOFQ Subcut (4) lantern templates per strip Total lantern pieces needed: 110	Per fat quarter: (3) 6½ in (16.5cm) x LOFQ Subcut (4) lantern templates per strip Total lantern pieces needed: 156	A
Fabric 2	(2) 1in (2.5cm) x WOF strips Cut (1) strip in half	(3) 1in (2.5cm) x WOF strips Cut (1) strip in half	(4) 1in (2.5cm) x WOF strips Cut (1) strip in half	(6) 1in (2.5cm) x WOF strips Cut (1) strip in half	B
Fabric 3	(4) 6¾in (17.2cm) x WOF strips Fold (see cutting instructions) Subcut (13) pairs Triangle Template per strip Total pairs of triangles needed: 42	(6) 6¾in (17.2cm) x WOF strips Fold (see cutting instructions) Subcut (13) pairs Triangle Template per strip Total pairs of triangles needed: 72	(9) 6¾in (17.2cm) x WOF strips Fold (see cutting instructions) Subcut (13) pairs Triangle Template per strip Total pairs of triangles needed: 110	(12) 6¾in (17.2cm) x WOF strips Fold (see cutting instructions) Subcut (13) pairs Triangle Template per strip Total pairs of triangles needed: 156	C
	(3) 3in (7.6cm) x WOF strips Cut (1) strip in half	(6) 3in (7.6cm) x WOF strips Cut (1) strip in half	(8) 3in (7.6cm) x WOF strips	(11) 3in (7.6cm) x WOF strips Cut (1) strip in half	D
	(7) 2½in (6.4cm) x WOF strips Sew strips end to end Subcut (5) 2½ x 51in (6.4 x 155cm)	(12) 2½in (6.4cm) x WOF strips Sew strips end to end Subcut (7) 2½ x 65½in (6.4 x 166.4cm)	(18) 2½in (6.4cm) x WOF strips Sew strips end to end Subcut (9) 2½ x 80in (6.4 x 203cm)	(26) 2½in (6.4cm) x WOF strips Sew strips end to end Subcut (11) 2½ x 90in (6.4 x 228.5cm)	E
	(3) 1½in (3.8cm) x WOF strips Sew strips end to end Subcut (2) 1½in x 51in (3.8 x 129.5cm)	(4) 1½in (3.8cm) x WOF strips Sew strips end to end Subcut (2) 1½in x 65½in (3.8 x 166.4cm)	(4) 1½in (3.8cm) x WOF strips Sew strips end to end Subcut (2) 1½in x 80in (3.8 x 203cm)	(5) 1½in (3.8cm) x WOF strips Sew strips end to end Subcut (2) 1½in x 90in (3.8 x 228.5cm)	F
Binding	(6) 2½in (6.4cm) strips	(7) 2½in (6.4cm) strips	(9) 2½in (6.4cm) strips	(10) 2½in (6.4cm) strips	

Note
- Please read through all the instructions before beginning.
- Fabric quantities assume a WOF of 42in (107cm).
- All seams have a ¼in (6mm) seam allowance.

Hot tip

The number of fat quarters shown for each size is the minimum number needed for that size. Use more in different colors for greater lantern variety, or for fussy cutting.

Cutting instructions

1. For the lanterns, cut two pieces from the same fabric for each lantern to get the shape, or cut a pair from different fabrics if you choose. The cutting list gives a letter label to each piece to help with organization and construction later. The cutting diagram below shows how many lantern pieces you can cut from one fat quarter of Fabric 1 in a single layer.

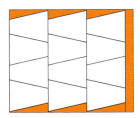

2. Cut the Fabric 3 WOF strips. Fold each strip across the middle with right sides together so you have a double layer piece that is 6½ x 21in (16.5 x 53.5cm). You will have a pair of mirrored triangles each time you cut. The cutting diagram shows you how many pairs of triangles you can cut from this piece.

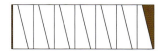

3. Measure and mark all other pieces using the quilting ruler and then cut them out with the rotary cutter and mat.

Hot tip

When cutting out follow the number of lantern pieces and pairs of triangles needed for the size you are making to avoid cutting too many and wasting fabric.

Chain block construction

4. Gather together all the B and D strips, and pair two D strips with each B strip. Place a B strip right sides together with the D strip and sew along one long edge. Open out and press the seams open. Repeat to add the other D strip on the other side. Each strip should measure 6in (15.3cm) as shown below.

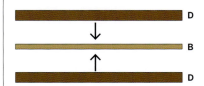

5. Cut each strip into smaller pieces—piece L will be 6 x 3in (15.3 x 7.6cm) and piece S will be 6 x 1½in (15.3 x 3.8cm). You will need the following for each size:

Piece L
- Small 18
- Medium 32
- Large 50
- Mega 72

Piece S
- Small 6
- Medium 8
- Large 10
- Mega 12

Lantern block construction

6 Gather together one A and a mirrored pair of C pieces. Fold each in half as shown by the green line and fingerpress to crease a fold to mark the center, then unfold.

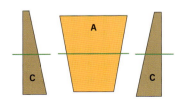

7 With right sides together and matching centers, sew the left piece C to the left side of piece A. Open out and press the seams open, then repeat to add the right piece C to the right side of piece A. Note that the C pieces will be slightly longer than the A piece, but this is correct.

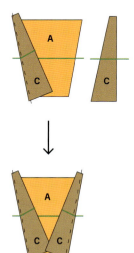

8 Trim the lantern unit as shown by the red lines. Each lantern unit should now be 6in (15.3cm) wide by 6½in (16.5cm) high.

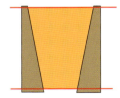

9 Repeat steps 6 to 8 until all the single lantern units are complete. To make a paired lantern unit, place two matching single lantern units right sides together and sew along the center line to join as shown. Press the seam open. Each paired lantern unit should now be 6in (15.3cm) wide by 12½in (31.8cm) high.

SINGLE LANTERN UNIT

PAIRED LANTERN UNIT

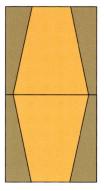

10 You will need the following for each size:

Single lantern unit
Small 6
Medium 8
Large 10
Mega 12

Paired lantern unit
Small 18
Medium 32
Large 50
Mega 72

Quilt construction

11 Lay out all the pieces for your chosen size to determine the placement for all the different color lanterns. First sew each lantern column together, using an S piece and a single lantern unit at one end and the number of paired lantern units and L pieces required for the size you are making.

12 When you have made all your lantern columns, add the E strips between them and then an F strip on each side.

13 When the quilt top is complete, refer to "Assembling your quilt" and choose your preferred methods to layer, quilt, and finish your quilt.

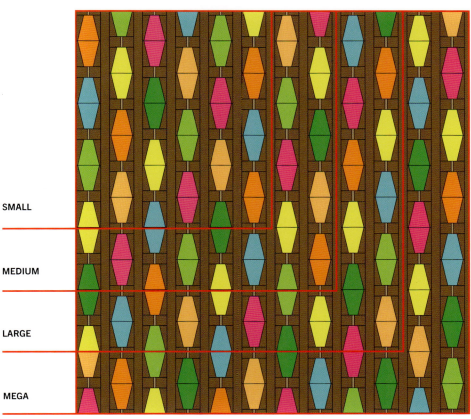

SMALL

MEDIUM

LARGE

MEGA

PATIO LANTERNS

61

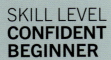

SKILL LEVEL
CONFIDENT BEGINNER

Outta Sight

Outta Sight showcases many elements of retro style, all in one quilt. Stripes, illusions, and color play combined make for serious retro vibes. The legendary David Bowie inspired this quilt—the repeating circles remind me of space, which features in several of his songs, and I have chosen a color palette that mimics his iconic Ziggy Stardust painted face.

Tools & Materials

- Rotary cutter
- Cutting mat
- Fabric shears (optional)
- Pins
- Sewing machine
- Thread to match fabrics
- Outta Sight circle template (see Templates)
- Stiletto or tweezers
- 6½ x 24in quilting ruler
- Metal straight edge
- Iron and ironing board
- Pillow form (if making pillow)

Fabric requirements

	Pillow	Small	Medium	Large
Finished size	20in (50.8cm) square	48 x 52in (121.9 x 132cm)	64 x 70in (162.5 x 177.8cm)	80 x 88in (203.2 x 223.5cm)
	1 block	3 rows of 3 blocks	4 rows of 4 blocks	5 rows of 5 blocks
Fabrics 1–8 (circles/background)	⅛ yard (11.4cm) each	⅝ yard (58cm) each	1 yard (91.4cm) each	1½ yards (137.2cm) each
Fabric 9 (darker tone of fabric 1)	⅛ yard (11.4cm)	¼ yard (22.9cm)	¼ yard (22.9cm)	⅓ yard (30.5cm)
Fabric 10 (darker tone of fabric 8)	⅛ yard (11.4cm)	¼ yard (22.9cm)	⅓ yard (30.5cm)	⅓ yard (30.5cm)
Lightweight fusible interfacing	½ yard (46cm)	2⅛ yard (194.3cm)	3½ yards (320cm)	5⅝ yards (514.4cm)
Backing (with 4in/10cm overage)	¾ yard (68.6cm)	2⅓ yards (213.4cm)	4⅓ yards (396.2cm)	6⅛ yards (560cm)
Batting/wadding (with 4in/10cm overage)	22in (55.9cm) square	1⅝ yards (148.6cm)	2 yards, 90in wide (183cm, 228.6cm wide)	2¾ yards, 90in wide (251.5cm, 228.6cm wide)
Binding (2½in/6.4cm strips)		½ yard (46cm)	⅝ yard (57.2cm)	⅔ yard (61cm)
Pillow back	½ yard (46cm)			

Cutting

	Pillow	Small	Medium	Large
Finished size	1 block	3 rows of 3 blocks	4 rows of 4 blocks	5 rows of 5 blocks
Fabrics 1–8	(1) 2½in (6.4cm) x WOF strip	(7) 2½in (6.4cm) x WOF strips	(12) 2½in (6.4cm) x WOF strips	(19) 2½in (6.4cm) x WOF strips
Fabric 9	(1) 2½in (6.4cm) x WOF strip Subcut (1) 2½ x 20½in (6.4 x 52cm)	(2) 2½in (6.4cm) x WOF strips	(2) 2½in (6.4cm) x WOF strips	(4) 2½in (6.4cm) x WOF strips
Fabric 10	(1) 2½in (6.4cm) x WOF strip Subcut (1) 2½ x 20½in (6.4 x 52cm)	(2) 2½in (6.4cm) x WOF strips	(4) 2½in (6.4cm) x WOF strips	(4) 2½in (6.4cm) x WOF strips
Pillow top backing	(1) 22in (56cm) x WOF strip Subcut (1) 22in (56cm) square			
Pillow back	(1) 13½in (34.3cm) x WOF strip Subcut (2) 13½ x 20½in (34.3 x 52cm)			
Lightweight fusible interfacing	(1) 15½in (39.4cm) square	(5) 15½in (39.4cm) squares	(8) 15½in (39.4cm) squares	(13) 15½in (39.4cm) squares
Binding		(6) 2½in (6.4cm) strips	(8) 2½in (6.4cm) strips	(9) 2½in (6.4cm) strips

Note

- Please read through all the instructions before beginning.
- Fabric quantities assume a WOF of 42in (107cm).
- Fusible web/interfacing quantities assume a WOF of 20in (51cm).
- All seams have a ¼in (6mm) seam allowance.

Cutting instructions

1 Using a rotary cutter and cutting mat, cut the pieces as listed in the cutting table for the size of project you are making.

Block construction

2 Gather all the WOF strips in fabrics 1–8 and arrange them in sets of 8 colors in numerical order. You will need 1 set for the **Pillow**, 7 sets for the **Small** quilt, 12 sets for the **Medium** quilt, and 19 sets for the **Large** quilt.

3 Place the first two strips right sides together and sew along one edge. Add the next strip in order but sew in the opposite direction to prevent the strips set from bowing. Continue adding strips in order, sewing in alternate directions each time until all the strips are joined. Press half the seams towards fabric 1 and the other half towards fabric 8. Repeat with all your sets of strips for the size you are making.

4 Cut the panels into blocks as follows:

Pillow	(1) 16½ x 20½in (42 x 52cm) block and (1) 16½ x 15½in (42 x 39.4cm) block
Small	(9) 16½in (42cm) square blocks and (5) 16½ x 15½in (42 x 39.4cm) blocks
Medium	(16) 16½in (42cm) square blocks and (8) 16½ x 15½in (42 x 39.4cm) blocks
Large	(25) 16½in (42cm) square blocks and (13) 16½ x 15½in (42 x 39.4cm) blocks

> **Hot tip**
> The pillow top backing will not be seen inside the pillow cover, so you could use a cheaper fabric such as muslin here.

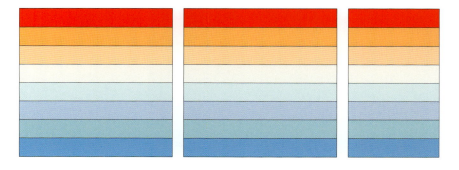

5 The 16½ x 15½in (42 x 39.4cm) blocks will all be cut into circles. Print and cut out the quarter-circle template. Fold the first one in half and then in half again. Place the quarter-circle template aligned with the folded edges and cut along the curved edge as shown in the diagram. Open out into a circle. Repeat for all blocks of this size to create the following:

Pillow	1 circle
Small	5 circles
Medium	8 circles
Large	13 circles

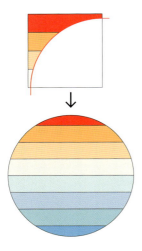

6 Cut a circle of fusible interfacing the same size as the fabric circle. Follow the Turned Edge Appliqué instructions in the Quilting Essentials chapter to prepare the circles.

7 Fold the circle and one of the square blocks in half vertically to find the center and fingerpress to crease. Place the circle on top of the square block, but rotated so the colors run in the other direction. Align the creases to center it and make sure the horizontal seams all match up. Fuse in place with a hot iron, then topstitch around the circle ⅛in (3mm) from the edge.

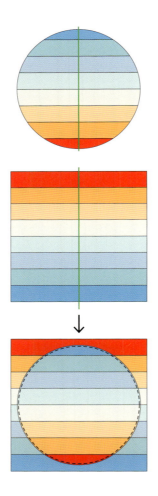

8 Repeat steps 6 and 7 to make the number of circle blocks you need for the size you are making. If you are making the pillow, the background for the circle will be the 16½ x 20½in (42 x 52cm) rectangular block.

Pillow construction

9 Add the 2½ x 20½in (5 x 52cm) strip in fabric 9 to the top of the pillow front and the 2½ x 20½in (6.4 x 52cm) strip in fabric 10 to the bottom. Press the seams in one direction.

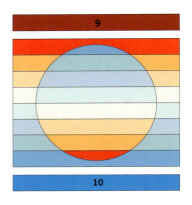

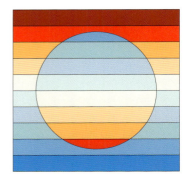

10 When the pillow top is complete, layer the top, batting, and backing and quilt.

11 Follow the Envelope Pillow Back instructions in "Quilting Essentials" to complete your pillow.

Quilt construction

12 Sew the 2½in (6.4cm) x WOF strip in fabric 9 end to end to make one long strip and then cut the following:

    Small   (1) 2½ x 48½in
                (6.4 x 123.3cm)
    Medium (1) 2½ x 64½in
                (6.4 x 164cm)
    Large   (2) 2½ x 80½in
                (6.4 x 204.5cm)

13 Sew the 2½in (6.4cm) x WOF strip in fabric 10 end to end to make one long strip and then cut the following:

    Small   (1) 2½ x 48½in
                (6.4 x 123.3cm)
    Medium (2) 2½ x 64½in
                (6.4 x 164cm)
    Large   (2) 2½ x 80½in
                (6.4 x 204.5cm)

14 Sew the circle and the square blocks together alternately to make the number of rows you need, following the diagram for the size you are making. Press alternate seams in opposite directions so they will nest. Sew the rows together, adding in the strips in fabric 9 and fabric 10 and flipping alternate rows to get the graded color effect. Press the seams open.

15 When the quilt top is complete, refer to "Assembling your quilt" and choose your preferred methods to layer, quilt, and finish your quilt.

PILLOW

SMALL

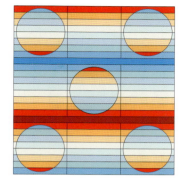

MEDIUM

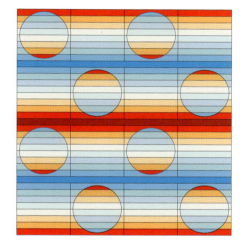

LARGE

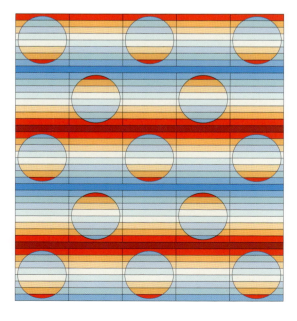

**SKILL LEVEL
CONFIDENT BEGINNER**

Flower Power

This style of flower was so popular in the late '60s and early '70s that I knew I had to have them in a pattern. Depending on how you look at things, you could make this more of an amoeba than a flower. This quilt is easy in that it's the same block throughout, just rotated to give some movement. Play around and make these melty tripping daisies your own.

Hot tip
For a different take on the flowers, try enlarging the centers, or even taking them away.

Tools & Materials
- Rotary cutter
- Cutting mat
- Flower Power templates (see Templates)
- Fabric shears (optional)
- Pins
- Iron and ironing board
- Sewing machine
- Thread to match fabrics
- 6½ x 24in quilting ruler
- Metal straight edge
- Pillow form (if making pillow)

Fabric requirements

	Pillow	Small	Medium	Large
Finished size	20in (50.8cm) square 1 block	51in (129.5cm) square 3 rows of 3 blocks	68in (172.7cm) square 4 rows of 4 blocks	85in (215.9cm) square 5 rows of 5 blocks
Single fabric background	(1) 20½in (52cm) square	2½ yards (228.6cm)	4 yards (365.8cm)	6½ yards (594.4cm)
Scrappy background		(9) Fat quarters	(16) Fat quarters	(25) Fat quarters
Single fabric flowers	(1) Fat quarter	2½ yards (228.6cm)	3¾ yard (342.9cm)	6 yards (548.6cm)
Scrappy flowers	(1) Fat quarter	(9) Fat quarters	(16) Fat quarters	(25) Fat quarters
Flower centers (optional)	(1) 2½ x 3½in (6.4cm x 8.9cm)	⅛ yard (11.4cm)	¼ yard (22.9cm)	¼ yard (22.9cm)
Pillow back fabric	¾ yard (68.6cm)			
Fusible web 20in (51cm) wide	½ yard (45.7cm)	4¼ yards (388.6cm)	7⅝ yards (697.2cm)	11⅝ yards (1063cm)
Backing (with 4in/10cm overage)	¾ yard (68.6cm)	3⅜ yards (308.6cm)	4¼ yards (388.6cm)	6⅜ yards (582.9cm)
Batting / wadding (with 4in/10cm overage)	¾ yard (68.6cm)	1⅔ yards, 60in wide (152.4cm, 152.4cm wide)	4¼ yards (388.6cm)	2⅝ yards, 120in wide (240cm, 304.7cm wide)
Binding (2½in/6.4cm strips)		½ yard (45.7cm)	⅝ yard (57.2cm)	⅔ yard (61cm)

Cutting

	Pillow	Small	Medium	Large
Finished size	1 block	3 rows of 3 blocks	4 rows of 4 blocks	5 rows of 5 blocks
Single fabric background	(1) 20½in (52cm) square	(5) 17½in (44.5cm) x WOF strips Subcut (9) 17½in (44.5cm) squares	(8) 17½in (44.5cm) x WOF strips Subcut (16) 17½in (44.5cm) squares	(13) 17½in (44.5cm) x WOF strips Subcut (25) 17½in (44.5cm) squares
Scrappy background		(1) 17½in (44.5cm) square from each fat quarter	(1) 17½in (44.5cm) square from each fat quarter	(1) 17½in (44.5cm) square from each fat quarter
Single fabric flowers	(1) 16¼in (41.3cm) x WOFQ	(5) 16¼in (41.3cm) x WOF strip Subcut (9) 16¼in (41.3cm) squares	(8) 16¼in (41.3cm) x WOF strip Subcut (16) 16¼in (41.3cm) squares	(13) 16¼in (41.3cm) x WOF strip Subcut (25) 16¼in (41.3cm) squares
Scrappy flowers	(1) 16¼in (41.3cm) square	(9) 16¼in (41.3cm) squares	(16) 16¼in (41.3cm) squares	(25) 16¼in (41.3cm) squares
Flower centers (optional)	(1) 2¼ x 3½in (5.8 x 8.9cm)	(1) 2¼in (5.8cm) x WOF strip	(2) 2¼in (5.8cm) x WOF strips	(3) 2¼in (5.8cm) x WOF strips
Pillow backing	(1) 22in (55.9cm) square			
Pillow back fabric	(2) 12½ x 21in (31.8 x 53.3cm)			
Fusible web 20in (51cm) wide – flowers	(1) 16¼in (41.3cm) square	(9) 16¼in (41.3cm) squares	(16) 16¼in (41.3cm) squares	(25) 16¼in (41.3cm) squares
Fusible web 20in (51cm) wide – flower centers (optional)	(1) 2¼ x 3¼in (5.7 x 8.3cm)	(2) 2¼in (5.7cm) x WOF	(4) 2¼in (5.7cm) x WOF	(5) 2¼in (5.7cm) x WOF
Binding		(6) 2½in (6.4cm) x WOF strips	(8) 2½in (6.4cm) x WOF strips	(9) 2½in (6.4cm) x WOF strips

Note
- Please read through all the instructions before beginning.
- Fabric quantities assume a WOF of 42in (107cm).
- Fusible web quantities assume a WOF of 20in (51cm).
- All seams have a ¼in (6mm) seam allowance.

Cutting instructions

1. Follow Steps 1–5 of the Raw Edge Appliqué instructions in the Quilting Essentials chapter.

2. If you want contrast flower centers, iron the 2in (5cm) fusible web strip to the wrong side of each flower center strip. Trace up to twelve flower center templates onto the paper backing of each fusible web strip. Carefully cut out each shape. If you want to have the background fabric as your flower center, also cut out the center oval shape in step 2 of the Raw Edge Appliqué instructions.

Block construction

3. Follow Steps 6 and 7 of the Raw Edge Appliqué instructions.

4. If you are adding contrast flower centers, remove the paper backing and position the flower centers on each flower then press to fuse in place.

5. Sew around the flower centers with a ⅛in (3mm) seam, using a zigzag or satin stitch, if desired.

Pillow construction

6. When the pillow top is complete, layer the top, batting and pillow backing and quilt using your preferred methods.

7. Follow the Envelope Pillow Back instructions in the Quilting Essentials chapter to complete your pillow.

Quilt construction

8. If you have made the scrappy version, lay out the blocks in rows to the size you are making and move them around until you are happy with the color arrangement.

9. Sew the blocks together to make the number of rows you need for the size you are making, pressing the seams in alternate directions.

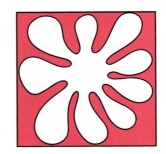

10 Sew the rows together. Iron the seams open or nest the seams, whatever technique is preferred.

11 When the quilt top is complete, please refer to "Assembling your quilt" for essential quilting techniques, and choose your preferred methods to layer, quilt, and finish your quilt.

Hot tip
Use different stitches or hand embroidery to embellish the centers of your flowers for more groovy fun.

PILLOW

SMALL

MEDIUM

LARGE

SKILL LEVEL
INTERMEDIATE

Checkered Adventure

There are two parts to this quilt—first you make up the gorgeous checkerboard background, using one of the four design options, then choose your appliqué pieces. You can use all the templates given, or just choose a few—or even just one to repeat over and over!

Tools & Materials

- Rotary cutter
- Cutting mat
- Checkered Adventure templates (see Templates)
- Fabric shears (optional)
- Pins
- Sewing machine
- Thread to match fabrics
- Stiletto or tweezers
- 6½ x 24in quilting ruler
- Metal straight edge
- Iron and ironing board
- Spray starch (optional)

Fabric requirements

Quilt	Small	Medium	Large	Mega
Finished size	48in (122cm) square	60in (152.5cm) square	72in (183cm) square	96in (243.8cm) square
	4 rows of 4 blocks	5 rows of 5 blocks	6 rows of 6 blocks	8 rows of 8 blocks
One color + scrappy	1¼ yards (114.3cm) main fabric Plus (5) Fat quarters	1¾ yards (160cm) main fabric Plus (7) Fat quarters	2½ yards (228.6cm) main fabric Plus (10) Fat quarters	4⅜ yards (400cm) main fabric Plus (18) Fat quarters
Two colors	1¼ yards (114.3cm) each color	1¾ yards (160cm) each color	2½ yards (228.6cm) each color	4⅜ yards (400cm) each color
Two color scrappy	(16) Fat quarters	(26) Fat quarters	(36) Fat quarters	(64) Fat quarters
Super scrappy	(9) Fat quarters	(14) Fat quarters	(20) Fat quarters	(35) Fat quarters
Backing (with 4in/10cm overage)	2⅓ yards (213.4cm)	3⅞ yards (354.3cm)	4½ yards (411.5cm)	8⅔ yards (792.5cm)
Batting/wadding (with 4in/10cm overage)	1⅝ yards, 60in wide (148.6cm, 152.4cm wide)	2 yards, 90 in wide (183cm, 228.6cm wide)	2¼ yards (205.7cm)	3 yards, 120in wide (274.3cm, 304.8cm wide)
Binding (2½in/6.4cm strips)	½ yard (45.7cm)	⅝ yard (57.2cm)	⅝ yard (57.2cm)	¾ yard (68.6cm)

Appliqué						
Group A templates	All Group A templates	Flower 1A only	Flower 2A only	Star 1A only	Star 2A only	Mushroom 1A only
Main fabric	1¾ yards (160cm)	(1) Fat quarter	(1) Fat quarter	(1) Fat quarter	(1) Fat quarter	(1) Fat quarter
Contrast fabric		8in (20.3cm) square	8in (20.3cm) square			2½ x 12in (6.4 x 30.5cm)
Fusible interfacing or web 20in (51cm) wide	2½ yards (228.6cm)	⅞ yard (80cm)	⅔ yard (61cm)	¾ yard (68.6cm)	¾ yard (68.6cm)	1 yard (91.4cm)
Group B templates	All Group B templates	Flower 3B only	Star 2B only			
Main fabric	½ yard (45.7cm)	(1) Fat quarter	(1) Fat quarter			
Contrast fabric		12in (30.5cm) square				
Fusible interfacing or web 20in (51cm) wide	1 yard (91.4cm)	¾ yard (68.6cm)	½ yard (45.7cm)			
Group C templates	All Group C templates	Flower 1C only	Star 1C only	Mushroom 1C only	Mushroom 2C only	
Main fabric	⅔ yard (61cm)	(1) Fat quarter	(1) Fat quarter	(3) Fat quarters	(3) Fat quarters	
Contrast fabric		5½in (14cm) square		2 x 8in (5 x 20.3cm)	2 x 6in (5 x 15cm)	
Fusible interfacing or web 20in (51cm) wide	1½ yards (136cm)	⅜ yard (35cm)	⅜ yard (35cm)	⅜ yard (35cm)	⅝ yard (57.1cm)	
Group D templates	All Group D templates	Flower 2D only	Flower 3D only	Star 1D only	Star 2D only	
Main fabric	⅓ yard (30.5cm)	10in (25.5cm) square	10in (25.5cm) square	10in (25.5cm) square	10in (25.5cm) square	
Contrast fabric		4in (10cm) square	5½in (14cm) square			
Fusible interfacing or web 20in (51cm) wide	½ yard (45.7cm)	10in (25.5cm) square	10in (25.5cm) square	10in (25.5cm) square	10in (25.5cm) square	

Cutting

Quilt	Small	Medium	Large	Mega
Finished size	4 rows of 4 blocks	5 rows of 5 blocks	6 rows of 6 blocks	8 rows of 8 blocks
One color + scrappy	(11) 3½in (8.9cm) x WOF strips	(17) 3½in (8.9cm) x WOF strips	(24) 3½in (8.9cm) x WOF strips	(43) 3½in (8.9cm) x WOF strips
	Subcut each strip in half	Subcut each strip in half	Subcut each strip in half	Subcut each strip in half
	(5) 3½in (8.9cm) x WOFQ strips from each fat quarter	(5) 3½in (8.9cm) x WOFQ strips	(5) 3½in (8.9cm) x WOFQ strips	(5) 3½in (8.9cm) x WOFQ strips*
	(22) strips	(34) strips	(48) strips	(86) strips
Two colors	(11) 3½in (8.9cm) x WOF strips from each color	(17) 3½in (8.9cm) x WOF strips	(24) 3½in (8.9cm) x WOF strips	(43) 3½in (8.9cm) x WOF strips
	Subcut each strip in half	Subcut each strip in half	Subcut each strip in half	Subcut each strip in half
Two color scrappy	(3) 3½in (8.9cm) x WOFQ strips from each fat quarter	(3) 3½in (8.9cm) x WOFQ strips	(3) 3½in (8.9cm) x WOFQ strips	(3) 3½in (8.9cm) x WOFQ strips
	(48) strips	(78) strips	(108) strips	(192) strips
Super scrappy	(5) 3½in (8.9cm) x WOFQ strips* from each fat quarter	(5) 3½in (8.9cm) x WOFQ strips	(5) 3½in (8.9cm) x WOFQ strips	(5) 3½in (8.9cm) x WOFQ strips*
	(44) strips	(68) strips	(96) strips	(172) strips
Binding (2½in/6.4cm strips)	(6) 2½in (6.4cm) strips	(7) 2½in (6.4cm) strips	(8) 2½in (6.4cm) strips	(10) 2½in (6.4cm) strips

*More strips may be cut than needed. Set extra strips aside for another project.

Note
- Please read through all the instructions before beginning.
- Fabric quantities assume a WOF of 42in (107cm).
- Fusible web/interfacing quantities assume a width of 20in (51cm).
- All seams have a ¼in (6mm) seam allowance.
- Templates for this project can be found in "Templates."

Cutting instructions
1. There are four variations for the checkerboard background, so choose which one to make and follow the fabric quantities and cutting instructions for that variation. Using a rotary cutter and cutting mat, cut the strips as detailed in the cutting table. If you decide to use yardage instead of fat quarters the strips do not need to be cut in half—you only need the correct total number of WOF strips, so 22 for the **Small** size, 34 for the **Medium** size, 48 for the **Large** size and 86 for the **Mega** size.

Hot tip
Use more fat quarters in the Super Scrappy version than stated for greater variety.

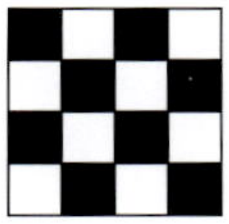

One color and Scrappy

Two colors

Two color Scrappy

Super Scrappy

Checkerboard construction

2 Gather four strips together as shown for the variation you are making.

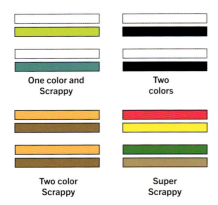

3 Place each pair of strips right sides together and sew along the long edge, then sew the pairs into a block of four strips. Alternate the sewing direction each time to avoid bowing. Press all the seams in one direction. Each strip set should measure 12½in (31.8cm) tall.

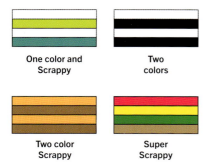

4 Measure and cut the strip set at 3½in (9cm) intervals. Each WOFQ strip set should yield six 3½ x 12½in (9 x 31.8cm) units. A full WOF strip will yield twelve 3½ x 12½in (9 x 31.8cm) units.

5 If you are making the One color + Scrappy variation or the Super scrappy variation, repeat steps 2–4 for additional units with varying colors.

6 Arrange four units as shown below for each variation. Note how the two colors alternate; the Scrappy versions can mix units. Making sure the horizontal seams are aligned each time, sew the units together. Press the seams open. A finished 4 x 4 checkerboard block should measure 12½ x 12½in (31.8 x 31.8cm).

One color and Scrappy

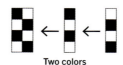
Two colors

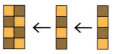
Two color Scrappy

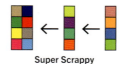
Super Scrappy

7 Repeat steps 2–6 until all the 4 x 4 checkerboard blocks are complete. You will need the following number of 4 x 4 blocks for each size:

Small 16
Medium 25
Large 36
Mega 64

8 Assemble the 4 x 4 blocks in sets of four, aligning seams and co-ordinating fabrics as shown below. To make each size you will need:

Small four 2 x 2 blocks
Medium four 2 x 2 blocks + nine single blocks
Large nine 2 x 2 blocks
Mega sixteen 2 x 2 blocks

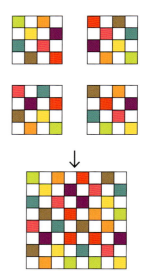

Applique instructions

9 Gather the appliqué pieces you need for your design and prepare them using the Turned Edge Appliqué method in the Quilting Essentials chapter. If there are smaller pieces that need to be layered on, such as a flower center or different parts for a mushroom, add them first.

10 Arrange the appliqué motifs right side up on the right side of the relevant 2 x 2 checkerboard block and press to fuse in place.

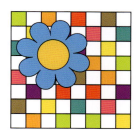

11 Sew ⅛in (3mm) from the edge around the motif or handsew in place.

12 Repeat to add appliqué motifs to any other blocks.

Quilt construction

13 Lay out the blocks in rows to the size you are making, then sew the rows together. Note that the **Medium** size will have nine single blocks that have not been sewn into 2 x 2 blocks Intersperse these between the 2 x 2 units in your layout.

14 Iron the seams open or nest the seams, whatever technique is preferred.

15 When the quilt top is complete, refer to "Assembling your quilt" and choose your preferred methods to layer, quilt, and finish your quilt.

Hot tip

If you are making one of the larger sizes, you will find it easier to lay out the 4 x 4 checkerboard blocks before joining them, so you can decide where to place your appliqué motifs on the overall background.

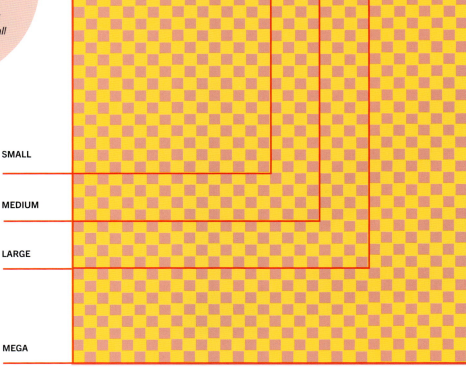

SMALL

MEDIUM

LARGE

MEGA

**SKILL LEVEL
INTERMEDIATE**

Op Art

Op Art is an abstract art style that creates optical illusions through repeating patterns and lines. The Op Art quilt was inspired by these artworks and by the Mod movement that began in London, England in the 1950s. In this quilt, Dresden Plate blocks are used to create a cool illusion effect that even beginners can achieve.

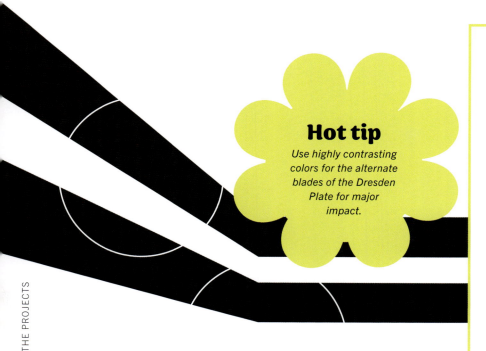

Hot tip
Use highly contrasting colors for the alternate blades of the Dresden Plate for major impact.

Tools & Materials
- Rotary cutter
- Cutting mat
- Small Dresden Blade template (see Templates)
- Dresden Center template (see Templates)
- Fabric shears (optional)
- Pins
- Fabric glue (if using the glue method for curves)
- Sewing machine
- Thread to match fabrics
- Pinking shears (optional)
- Stiletto or tweezers
- Non-stick silicone ironing mat, or parchment/freezer/wax paper
- 8½ x 8½in quilting ruler
- 6½ x 24in quilting ruler
- Iron and ironing board

Fabric requirements

	Small	Medium	Large	Mega
Finished size	40 x 48in (101.5 x 122cm) 6 rows of 5 blocks	56 x 64in (142.5 x 162.5cm) 8 rows of 7 blocks	72 x 80in (183 x 203cm) 10 rows of 19 blocks	88 x 96in (223.5 x 244cm) 12 rows of 11 blocks
Traditional version (2 colors)				
Fabric 1	2 yards (182.9cm)	3½ yards (320cm)	5½ yards (502.9cm)	7⅞ yards (720cm)
Fabric 2	2¼ yards (205.7cm)	4¼ yards (388.6cm)	6¼ yards (571.5cm)	9 yards (823cm)
Scrappy version				
Fabric 1	(30) 10in (25.4cm) squares or (9) Fat quarters	(56) 10in (25.4cm) squares or (16) Fat quarters	(90) 10in (25.4cm) squares or (25) Fat quarters	(132) 10in (25.4cm) squares or (37) Fat quarters
Fabric 2	2¼ yards (205.7cm)	4¼ yards (388.6cm)	6¼ yards (571.5cm)	9 yards (823cm)
Both versions				
Backing (with 4in/10cm overage)	2 yards (182.9cm)	3⅝ yards (331.5cm)	6¼ yards (571.5cm)	7¼ yards (662.9cm)
Batting/wadding (with 4in/10cm overage)	1⅓ yards, 60in wide (121.9cm, 152.4cm wide)	1⅞ yards, 60in wide (171.5cm, 152.4cm wide)	2¼ yards, 90in wide (205.7cm, 228.6cm wide)	2⅔ yards, 120in wide (243.8cm, 304.8cm wide)
Binding (2½in/6.4cm strips)	⅜ yard (34.3cm)	⅝ yard (57.2cm)	⅝ yard (57.2cm)	¾ yard (68.6cm)
Fusible interfacing 20in (51cm) wide	⅝ yard (57.2cm)	1¼ yards (114.3cm)	1⅞ yards (171.5cm)	2¾ yards (251.5cm)

Cutting

	Small	Medium	Large	Mega
Finished size	6 rows of 5 blocks	8 rows of 7 blocks	10 rows of 9 blocks	12 rows of 11 blocks
WOF				
Traditional Fabric 1 & 2 or Scrappy Fabric 2	(13) 5in (12.7cm) x WOF Subcut (300) blades	(24) 5in (12.7cm) x WOF Subcut (560) blades	(38) 5in (12.7cm) x WOF Subcut (900) blades	(55) 5in (12.7cm) x WOF Subcut (1320) blades
Traditional or Scrappy Fabric 2	(3) 3½in (8.9cm) x WOF Subcut (30) circles	(5) 3½in (8.9cm) x WOF Subcut (56) circles	(8) 3½in (8.9cm) x WOF Subcut (90) circles	(11) 3½in (8.9cm) x WOF Subcut (132) circles
Fusible interfacing	(6) 3½in (8.9cm) x WOF Subcut (30) circles	(12) 3½in (8.9cm) x WOF Subcut (56) circles	(18) 3½in (8.9cm) x WOF Subcut (90) circles	(27) 3½in (8.9cm) x WOF Subcut (132) circles
Each fat quarter				
Scrappy fabric 1	(3) 5in (12.7cm) x WOFQ Subcut (12) blades per strip (300) blades	(3) 5in (12.7cm) x WOFQ Subcut (12) blades per strip (560) blades	(3) 5in (12.7cm) x WOFQ Subcut (12) blades per strip (900) blades	(3) 5in (12.7cm) x WOFQ Subcut (12) blades per strip (1320) blades
Each 10in (25cm) strip	(2) 5in (12.7cm) strips Subcut (5) blades per strip (300) blades	(2) 5in (12.7cm) strips Subcut (5) blades per strip (560) blades	(2) 5in (12.7cm) strips Subcut (5) blades per strip (900) blades	(2) 5in (12.7cm) strips Subcut (5) blades per strip (1320) blades
Binding	(5) 2½in (6.4cm) strips	(7) 2½in (6.4cm) strips	(8) 2½in (6.4cm) strips	(10) 2½in (6.4cm) strips

Note
- Please read through all the instructions before beginning.
- Fabric quantities assume a WOF of 42in (107cm).
- An 18-degree Dresden ruler could be used in place of the Op Art Dresden template. Cut at 5in (12.7cm) mark.
- All seams have a ¼in (6mm) seam allowance.

Cutting instructions

1. Using a rotary cutter and cutting mat, cut 5in (12.7cm) x WOF strips from both Fabric 1 and Fabric 2. Subcut the strips into Dresden Plate blades by rotating the Small Dresden Blade template by 180 degrees after each cut. Follow the cutting diagrams below if you are using fat quarters or 10in (25cm) squares. Each Dresden Plate block will require 20 blades—ten in each color—so if you are making the **Small** version with six rows of five blocks (30 blocks in total) you will need 300 blades in Fabric 1 and 300 blades in Fabric 2. For a **Medium** version you need 56 blocks, for a **Large** 90 blocks, and for the **Mega** 132 blocks.

WOF

WOFQ

10in (25cm) SQUARE

2. From Fabric 2 cut 3½in (9cm) x WOF fabric strips. Subcut circles using the Dresden Center template. Each Dresden Plate block needs one circle center so for the **Small** version you will need 30, for a **Medium** version you will need 56, for a **Large** 90, and for the **Mega** 132.

3. From the fusible interfacing cut 3½in (9cm) x WOF fabric strips. Subcut circles using the Dresden Circle template. Again, for the **Small** version you will need 30, for a **Medium** version you will need 56, for a **Large** version 90, and for the **Mega** version 132.

Dresden Plate construction

4. Gather all the blades together for the size of quilt you are making and follow the Dresden plate wedge blade instructions that are given in the Quilting Essentials chapter.

5. Make one Dresden Plate for each block that you need for the size of quilt you are making. Press each blade flat.

Making the Dresden Plate center

6. Place a circle of fabric and a circle of fusible interfacing right sides together, so the fusible side is facing inward.

7. Sew around the circle, ¼in (6mm) from the edge, backstitching at beginning and end.

8. Notch the seam allowance all around the edge or use pinking shears to remove bulk, so the curves will be smooth when turned right sides out.

9. Follow steps 6–7 of Turned Edge Fusible Appliqué in the Quilting Essentials chapter.

10. Once you are happy with the position, use a hot iron to fuse the center circle to the Dresden Plate block following the manufacturer's instructions for the fusible batting.

11. Repeat steps 6–10 to make a Dresden Plate center for each of the blocks.

Hot tip
You could appliqué the center circle using satin stitch or blanket stitch, working in bright colors for a funky effect!

Squaring up the Dresden Plate blocks

12 Fold the Dresden Plate block in half in both directions, making sure the fold runs down the center of an opposite pair of blades each time, and fingerpress the folds to crease them.

13 Unfold the block and align the 4¼in marks on an 8½in square quilting ruler with the creased lines. Use the rotary cutter to cut off the edges all around to make the round plate into an 8½in (21.6cm) square.

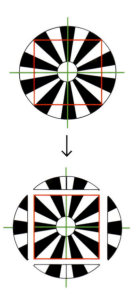

14 Repeat steps 12 and 13 for all the remaining blocks.

Quilt construction

15 If you have made the scrappy version, lay out the blocks in rows to the size you are making and move them around until you are happy with the color arrangement. You could use the diagram opposite for inspiration.

16 Sew the blocks together to make the number of rows you need for the size you are making.

17 Sew the rows together.

18 Iron the seams open or nest the seams as preferred.

19 When the quilt top is complete, baste, quilt, and bind. (See "Assembling your quilt" for tips on how to finish your quilt.)

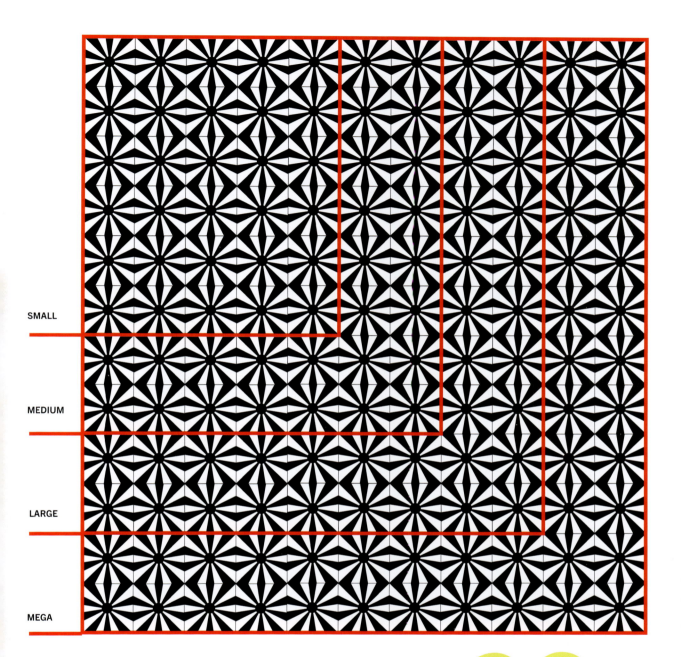

SMALL

MEDIUM

LARGE

MEGA

Scrappy inspiration

Hot tip
Make sure to align the cuts exactly the same for each block to achieve the optical illusion when you complete you quilt top.

SKILL LEVEL
INTERMEDIATE

Appliqué Adventure

Bring some retro goodness into your home with these Appliqué Adventure projects. I have noted which motifs I used to create my projects in the following instructions, but you don't have to copy me exactly. Mix and match the star, flower, and mushroom templates to create your own groovy designs.

Tools & Materials

- Rotary cutter
- Cutting mat
- Appliqué Adventure templates (see Templates)
- Fabric shears (optional)
- Pins
- Sewing machine
- Thread to match fabrics
- Spray starch (optional)
- 6½ x 24in quilting ruler
- Metal straight edge
- Iron and ironing board
- Pillow form (if making pillow)
- Approx 20in (51cm) wooden dowel (if making wall hanging)

Fabric requirements

For Star placemats or to add to a table/bed runner, you will not need the fusible interfacing listed for that appliqué shape.

Group A templates	All Group A templates	Flower 1A only	Flower 2A only	Star 1A only	Star 2A only	Mushroom 1A only
Main fabric	1¾ yards (160cm)	(1) Fat quarter	(1) Fat quarter	(1) Fat quarter	(1) Fat quarter	(3) Fat quarters
Contrast fabric		8in (20.3cm) square	8in (20.3cm) square			2½ x 12in (6.4 x 30.5cm)
Fusible interfacing 20in (51cm) wide	2½ yards (228.6cm)	⅞ yard (80cm)	⅔ yard (61cm)	¾ yard (68.6cm)	¾ yard (68.6cm)	1 yard (91.4cm)
Group B templates	**All Group B templates**	**Flower 3B only**	**Star 2B only**			
Main fabric	½ yard (45.7cm)	(1) Fat quarter	(1) Fat quarter			
Contrast fabric		12in (30.5cm) square				
Fusible interfacing 20in (51cm) wide	1 yard (91.4cm)	¾ yard (68.6cm)	½ yard (46cm)			
Group C templates	**All Group C templates**	**Flower 1C only**	**Star 1C only**	**Mushroom 1C only**	**Mushroom 2C only**	
Main fabric	⅔ yard (61cm)	(1) Fat quarter	(1) Fat quarter	(1) Fat quarter	(3) Fat quarters	
Contrast fabric		5½in (14cm) square		2 x 8in (5 x 20.3cm)	2 x 6in (5 x 15.2cm)	
Fusible interfacing 20in (51cm) wide	1½ yards (136cm)	⅜ yard (34.3cm)	⅜ yard (34.3cm)	⅜ yard (34.3cm)	⅝ yard (57.2cm)	
Group D templates	**All Group D templates**	**Flower 2D only**	**Flower 3D only**	**Star 1D only**	**Star 2D only**	
Main fabric	⅓ yard (30.5cm)	10in (25.4cm) square	10in (25.4cm) square	10in (25.4cm) square	10in (25.4cm) square	
Contrast fabric		4in (10cm) square	5½in (14cm) square			
Fusible interfacing 20in (51cm) wide	½ yard (45.7cm)	10in (25.4cm) square	10in (25.4cm) square	10in (25.4cm) square	10in (25.4cm) square	
Pillow	**Size 1**	**Size 2**	**Size 3**	**Size 4**		
Finished size	**24in (61cm) square**	**20in (51cm) square**	**16in (40.6cm) square**	**12in (30.5cm) square**		
Background fabric	¾ yard (68.6cm)	⅔ yard (61cm)	½ yard (45.7cm)	½ yard (45.7cm)		
Backing	¾ yard (68.6cm)	⅔ yard (61cm)	½ yard (45.7cm)	½ yard (45.7cm)		
Batting/fusible fleece	¾ yard (68.6cm)	⅔ yard (61cm)	½ yard (45.7cm)	½ yard (45.7cm)		
Pillow back	¾ yard (68.6cm)	⅔ yard (61cm)	½ yard (45.7cm)	⅜ yard (34.3cm)		
Wall hanging						
Finished size	(21 x 36in (53.5 x 91.5cm)					
Background fabric	⅔ yard (61cm)					
Backing	⅔ yard (61cm)					
Batting/fusible fleece	⅔ yard (61cm)					
Placemat	**Various sizes**					
Background fabric	(1) Fat quarter					
Backing	½ yard (45.7cm)					
Batting/fusible fleece	½ yard (45.7cm)					
Table/bed runner	**Small**	**Medium**	**Large**	**Mega**		
Finished size	**12 x 36in (30.5 x 91.4cm)**	**15 x 54in (38.1 x 137.2cm)**	**18 x 72in (45.8 x 182.9cm)**	**21 x 83in (53.3 x 210.8cm)**		
Background fabric	½ yard (45.7cm)	1 yard (91.4cm)	1¼ yards (114.3cm)	1¼ yards (114.3cm)		
Backing	½ yard (45.7cm)	1¼ yards (114.3cm)	1⅜ yards (125.7cm)	2¼ yards (205.7cm)		
Batting/fusible fleece	16½ x 40½in (42 x 102.9cm)	19½ x 58½in (49.5 x 148.6cm)	1⅜ yards (125.7cm)	2¼ yards (205.7cm)		
Binding (2½in/6.4cm strips)	¼ yard (23cm)	⅓ yard (30.5cm)	⅜ yard (34.3cm)	½ yard (45.7cm)		

Cutting

Pillow	Design A	Design B	Design C	Design D
Finished size	24in (61cm) square	20in (51cm) square	16in (40.6cm) square	12in (30.5cm) square
Background fabric	(1) 25in (63.5cm) square	(1) 21in (53.3cm) square	(1) 17in (43.2cm) square	(1) 13in (33cm) square
Backing	(1) 29in (73.7cm) square	(1) 25in (63.5cm) square	(1) 21in (53.3cm) square	(1) 17in (43.2cm) square
Batting/fusible fleece	(1) 29in (73.7cm) square	(1) 25in (63.5cm) square	(1) 21in (53.3cm) square	(1) 17in (43.2cm) square
Pillow back	(2) 15½ x 24in (39.4 x 61cm)	(2) 13½ x 20in (34.3 x 51cm)	(2) 11½ x 16in (29.3 x 40.6cm)	(2) 9½ x 12in (24.3 x 30.5cm)
Wall hanging				
Finished size	21 x 36in (53.3 x 91.4cm)			
Background fabric	(1) 21½ x 36½in (54.6 x 92.8cm)			
Backing	(1) 21½ x 36½in (54.6 x 92.8cm) and (2) 3½in (9cm) squares			
Batting/fusible fleece	(1) 21½ x 36½in (54.6 x 92.8cm)			
Table/bed runner	Small	Medium	Large	Mega
Finished size	12 x 36in (30.5 x 91.5cm)	15 x 54in (38.1 x 137.2cm)	18 x 72in (45.8 x 182.9cm)	21 x 83in (53.3 x 210.8cm)
Background fabric	(1) 12½in (31.8cm) x WOF	(2) 15½in (39.4cm) x WOF	(2) 18½in (47cm) x WOF	(2) 21½in (54.6cm) x WOF
Backing	(1) 16½in (42cm) x WOF Subcut (1) 16½ x 40½in (42 x 102.9cm)	(2) 19½in (49.5cm) x WOF Sew into 1 strip Subcut (1) 19½ x 58½in (49.5 x 148.5cm)	(2) 22½in (57.2cm) x WOF Sew into 1 strip Subcut (1) 22½ x 76½in (57.2 x 194.3cm)	(3) 25½in (64.8cm) x WOF Sew into 1 strip Subcut (1) 25½ x 88½in (64.8 x 224.8cm)
Batting/fusible fleece	(1) 16½in (42cm) x WOF Subcut (1) 16½ x 40½in (42 x 102.9cm)	(2) 19½in (49.5cm) x WOF Sew into 1 strip Subcut (1) 19½ x 58½in (49.5 x 148.5cm)	(2) 22½in (57.2cm) x WOF Sew into 1 strip Subcut (1) 22½ x 76½in (57.2 x 194.3cm)	(3) 25½in (64.8cm) x WOF Sew into 1 strip Subcut (1) 25½ x 88½in (64.8 x 224.8cm)
Binding (2½in/6.4cm strips)	(3) 2½in (6.4cm) x WOF strips	(4) 2½in (6.4cm) x WOF strips	(5) 2½in (6.4cm) x WOF strips	(6) 2½in (6.4cm) x WOF strips

Note
- Please read through all the instructions before beginning.
- Fabric quantities assume a WOF of 42in (107cm).
- Fusible web/interfacing quantities assume a WOF of 20in (51cm).
- All seams have a ¼in (6mm) seam allowance.
- The size of the placemats will vary depending on the template/design you choose.

▶ Pillow cutting instructions

1 The pillows can be made in four sizes: Design A uses Flower 2A template, Design B uses Flower 2B template, Design C uses Star 1C template and Design D uses Flower 3D template.

If you wish to use different templates, cut the background fabric to size based on the template you have chosen.

Only one template will be used on the front of the pillow.

Hot tip
You could make the pillow round instead of square—see the instructions for Round/Shaped Pillow Back.

APPLIQUÉ ADVENTURE

Pillow appliqué

2. Gather the appliqué pieces you need for your design and prepare them using the Turned Edge Appliqué method from the Quilting Essentials chapter. If there are smaller pieces that need to be layered on, such as a flower center or different parts for a mushroom, add them first.

Group A

Group B

Group C

Group D

3. When the appliqué design is complete, iron each piece in place onto the background fabric. Sew around the edges using topstitching ⅛in (3mm) from the edge, or hand sew in place with hidden stitches.

Pillow top quilting and construction

4. When the pillow top is complete, layer the top, batting and backing and quilt using your preferred methods.

5. Follow the Envelope Pillow Back instructions in the Quilting Essentials chapter to complete your pillow.

▶ Placemat cutting instructions

1. The placemat uses the Flower 3B template. If you wish to use a different template or make each mat different, cut the background fabric to size based on the templates you have chosen. Next, cut the appliqué pieces out.

Placemat appliqué

2. Gather the appliqué pieces you need for your design. If there are smaller pieces that need to be layered on, add them using the Turned Edge Appliqué method in the Quilting Essentials chapter.

Placemat construction and quilting

3. Lay the completed appliqué right side down on the fusible fleece and trace around it.

4. Cut out the shape from the fusible fleece and iron it onto the wrong side of the appliqué, following the manufacturer's instructions.

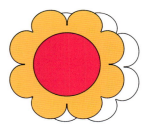

5. Lay the completed appliqué right side down on the backing fabric and trace around it. Cut the shape out.

6 Place the appliqué piece and the backing fabric right sides together, aligning all edges.

7 Sew all around the edge with an ⅛in (3mm) seam allowance, leaving a small gap on one side for turning.

8 Turn the mat right sides out and quilt using your preferred methods.

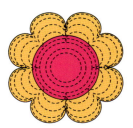

Hot tip
You can use these instructions to make a placemat, coaster, or table topper—just enlarge your chosen template to the size of the item you want to make.

▶ Wall hanging cutting instructions

1. The wall hanging uses Flower 3B template, Flower 1C template, Star 1C template, and Star 1D template. If you wish to use different templates, cut the background fabric to size based on the templates you have chosen. Cut the appliqué pieces out.

Wall hanging appliqué

2. Gather the appliqué pieces you need for your design and prepare them using the Turned Edge Appliqué method. If there are smaller pieces that need to be layered on, such as a flower center or different parts for a mushroom, add them first.

3. When the appliqué design is complete, iron each piece in place onto the background fabric. Sew around the edges using topstitching 1/8in (3mm) from the edge, or hand sew in place with hidden stitches.

4. Follow the manufacturer's instructions to iron the fusible batting or fleece onto the wrong side of the wall hanging.

Wall hanging quilting

5. Quilt the wall hanging using your preferred methods.

Wall hanging construction

6. Lay the quilted top right sides together on the backing rectangle. Sew around the edges 1/4in (6mm) from the edge, leaving a 4in (10cm) opening for turning and backstitching at the beginning and end.

7. Clip the corners and turn right sides out.

8. Top stitch around the edge of the wall hanging 1/8in (3mm) from the edge, enclosing the opening, and backstitching at the beginning and end.

9. See "Making a wall hanging" for instructions on adding hanging corners and finishing your wall hanging.

Hot tip

Add a fun trim such as pompoms or fringing along the bottom of your wall hanging!

▶Table/Bed runner cutting instructions

1. The runner uses Flower 1C template and Star 1A template. If you wish to use different templates, cut the background fabric to size based on the templates you have chosen. Cut the appliqué pieces out.

Table/Bed runner background and quilting instruction

2. Layer the backing fabric wrong side up, with the batting on top and the background fabric right side up on top of that. Refer to "Assembling your quilt" and choose your preferred methods to quilt.

3. Trim to size, leaving an extra ¼in (6mm) for the seam allowance and then bind.

Table/Bed runner background appliqué instruction

4. Gather the appliqué pieces you need for your design and the size of runner you are making. If there are smaller pieces that need to be layered on, add them using the Turned Edge Appliqué method.

5. Follow steps 3–8 of the placemat to make up as many appliqué motifs as desired.

6. Position the appliqué motifs on the runner—they do not need to be entirely on it but can overhang in places for a more dynamic design. When you have an arrangement you like, glue the motifs in place. Sew around the edge of each motif with a ⅛in (3mm) seam allowance.

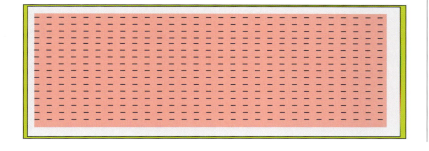

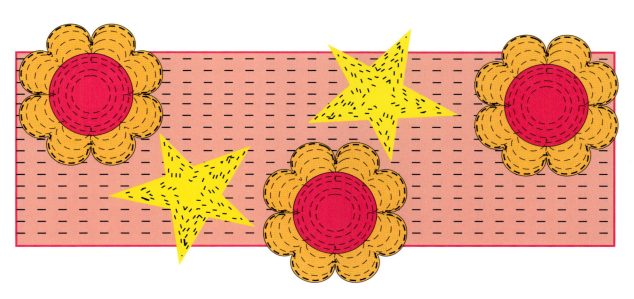

SKILL LEVEL
ADVANCED

Trippy Dippy

You can't think retro without thinking of some sort of trippy graphic—and this quilt epitomizes psychedelic trippy dippy cool, but in quilt form. Made in two contrasting colors, this quilt will be striking in any space—and, of course, trippy. Use one highly patterned fabric for even more contrast!

Tools & Materials

- Rotary cutter
- Cutting mat
- Trippy Dippy Templates A and B (see Templates)
- Water-soluble marker pen
- 6½ x 24in quilting ruler
- Metal straight edge
- Pins
- Fabric shears (optional)
- Fabric glue (if using the glue method for curves)
- Sewing machine
- Thread to match fabrics
- Stiletto or tweezers
- Iron and ironing board

Fabric requirements

	Small	Medium	Large	Mega
Finished size	45in (114.3cm) square (16) Block A, (16) Block B	64in (162.5cm) square (30) Block A, (30) Block B	76in (193cm) square (42) Block A, (42) Block B	96in (244cm) square (64) Block A, (64) Block B
Fabric 1	2¼ yards (205.7cm)	4 yards (365.8cm)	5¼ yards (480cm)	7¾ yards (708.7cm)
Fabric 2	2¼ yards (205.7cm)	4 yards (365.8cm)	5¼ yards (480cm)	7¾ yards (708.7cm)
Backing (with 4in/10cm overage)	2¼ yards (205.7cm)	4 yards (365.8cm)	4⅔ yards (426.7cm)	8¾ yards (800cm)
Batting/wadding (with 4in/10cm overage)	1½ yards, 60in wide (137.2cm, 152.4cm wide)	2 yards, 90in wide (182.9cm, 228.6cm wide)	2⅓ yards, 90in wide (213.4cm, 228.6cm wide)	3 yards, 120in wide (274.3cm, 304.8cm wide)
Binding (2½in/6.4cm strips)	⅜ yard (34.3cm)	⅝ yard (57.2cm)	⅝ yard (57.2cm)	¾ yard (68.6cm)

Cutting

	Small	Medium	Large	Mega
Finished size	(32) unit 1, (32) unit 2	(60) unit 1, (60) unit 2	(84) unit 1, (84) unit 2	(128) unit 1, (128) unit 2
Fabric 1	(4) 9½in (24.1cm) x WOF strips	(8) 9½in (24.1cm) x WOF strips	(11) 9½in (24.1cm) x WOF strips	(16) 9½in (24.1cm) x WOF strips
	Subcut (32) Template A	Subcut (60) Template A	Subcut (84) Template A	Subcut (128) Template A
	(4) 7½in (19cm) x WOF strips	(8) 7½in (19cm) x WOF strips	(11) 7½in (19cm) x WOF strips	(16) 7½in (19cm) x WOF strips
	Subcut (32) Template B	Subcut (60) Template B	Subcut (84) Template B	Subcut (128) Template B
Fabric 2	(4) 9½in (24.1cm) x WOF strips	(8) 9½in (24.1cm) x WOF strips	(11) 9½in (24.1cm) x WOF strips	(15) 9½in (24.1cm) x WOF strips
	Subcut (32) Template A	Subcut (60) Template A	Subcut (84) Template A	Subcut (128) Template A
	(4) 7½in (19cm) x WOF strips	(8) 7½in (19cm) x WOF strips	(11) 7½in (19cm) x WOF strips	(16) 7½in (19cm) x WOF strips
	Subcut (32) Template B	Subcut (60) Template B	Subcut (84) Template B	Subcut (128) Template B
Binding	(5) 2½in (6.4cm) strips	(7) 2½in (6.4cm) strips	(8) 2½in (6.4cm) strips	(10) 2½in (6.4cm) strips

Note
- Please read through all the instructions before beginning.
- Fabric quantities assume a WOF of 42in (107cm).
- All seams have a ¼in (6mm) seam allowance.

Cutting instructions
1. Trace Templates A and B onto both fabrics using the water-soluble pen and cut out with a rotary cutter or scissors.

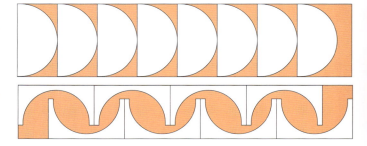

Template A

Template B

Hot tip
Stack as many WOF strips as you are comfortable cutting at once, aligning the edges. Pin your template to the strips and cut more than one at a time.

3   Sew the units together to make blocks. Each block should measure 9½ x 9½in (24 x 24cm). You will need the following for each size quilt:

Small	16 of each block
Medium	30 of each block
Large	42 of each block
Mega	64 of each block

BLOCK A

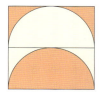

BLOCK B

Quilt construction

4   Assemble the diagonal rows as per the diagram for the size you are making (see overleaf), paying close attention to the orientation of the blocks. Each block should have the same block next to it but facing in the opposite direction. With right sides together, sew each pair of blocks into a row. Press the seams in opposite directions.

Block Construction

2   Follow the Half-circle technique given in the Quilting Essentials chapter to make the units. Press the seams to the Template B side. Trim all units to 5 x 9½in (12.7 x 24cm), making sure to leave ¼in (6mm) on both sides and top of the circle.

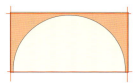

You will need the following for each size quilt:

Small	32 of each unit
Medium	60 of each unit
Large	84 of each unit
Mega	128 of each unit

UNIT 1

UNIT 2

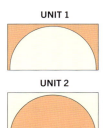

NOTE
For this pattern to work, you must create square blocks. That means each half-circle needs to measure half of the block size. Since your blocks finish at 9in (23cm) wide (9½in/24cm unfinished) the final block should be 9 x 9in (23 x 23cm) or 9½ x 9½in (24 x 24cm) unfinished.

5   Sew the rows together, matching the centers of the rows and nesting the seams. It is best to start in the center where the longest rows will be. Press the seams open.

6   Trim the edges of the quilt top by aligning a straight edge with the inner points of each side, then trimming away the excess points as shown below.

7   Please refer to "Assembling your quilt" to choose your preferred methods to layer, quilt, and finish your quilt.

SMALL

MEDIUM

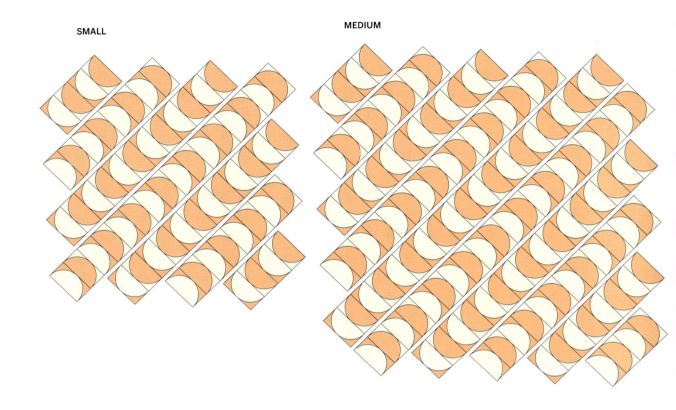

LARGE

MEGA

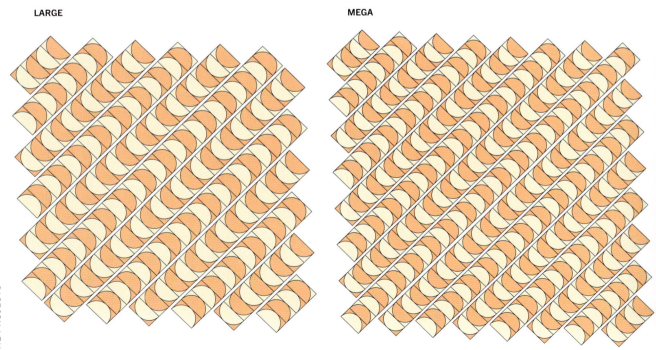

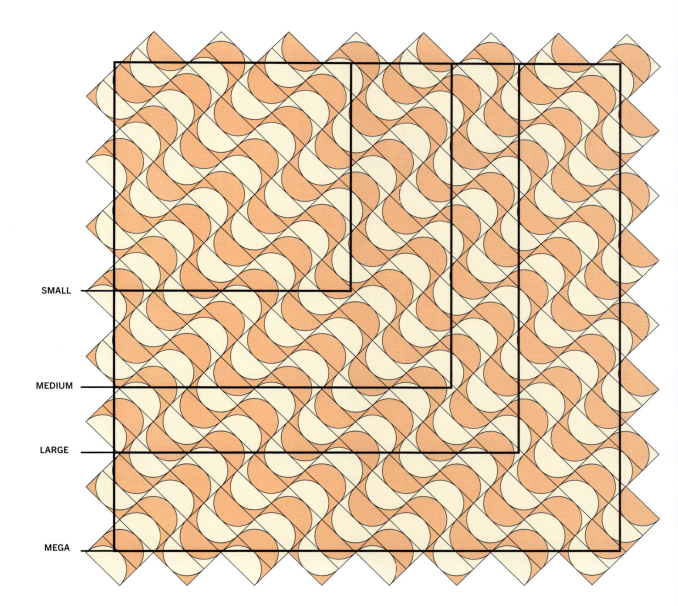

SKILL LEVEL
ADVANCED

Quilt 54

Andy Warhol and his art is synonymous with the '70s era, and I wanted to convey some of his style in a quilt. The Quilt 54 pattern uses color blocking and plays with value as a nod to the famous pop artist, giving the quilt both a modern and nostalgic feel.

Tools & Materials

- Rotary cutter
- Cutting mat
- Retro Blooms Small Template A and B (see Templates)
- Fabric shears (optional)
- Pins
- Fabric glue (if using the glue method for curves)
- Sewing machine
- Thread to match fabrics
- Stiletto or tweezers
- 6½ x 24in quilting ruler
- Metal straight edge
- Iron and ironing board
- Spray starch (optional)

Fabric requirements

	Small	Medium	Large	Mega
Finished size	48in (122cm) square 3 rows of 3 blocks	64in (162.5cm) square 4 rows of 4 blocks	80in (203.2cm) square 5 rows of 5 blocks	96in (243.8cm) square 6 rows of 6 blocks
Petal fabric	¾ yard (68.6cm) each of (3) colors	1 yard (91.4cm) each of (4) colors	1¼ yards (114.3cm) each of (5) colors	1 yard (91.4cm) each of (9) colors
Background fabrics	½ yard (45.7cm) each of (3) colors	⅝ yard (57.2cm) each of (4) colors	⅝ yard (57.2cm) each of (5) colors	⅝ yard (57.2cm) each of (9) colors
Center fabrics	⅜ yard (34.3cm) each of (3) colors	⅜ yard (34.3cm) each of (4) colors	½ yard (45.7cm) each of (5) colors	⅜ yard (34.3cm) each of (9) colors
Backing (with 4in/10cm overage)	2⅓ yards (213.4cm)	4 yards (365.8cm)	6¼ yards (571.5cm)	8⅔ yards (792.5cm)
Batting/wadding (with 4in/10cm overage)	1⅝ yards, 60in wide (148.6cm, 152.4cm wide)	2 yards, 90in wide (182.9cm, 228.6cm wide)	2½ yards, 90in wide (228.6cm, 228.6cm wide)	3 yards, 120in wide (274.3cm, 304.8cm wide)
Binding (2½in/6.4cm strips)	½ yard (45.7cm)	⅝ yard (57.2cm)	⅔ yard (61cm)	¾ yard (68.6cm)

Cutting

	Small	Medium	Large	Mega	Piece label
Finished size	3 rows of 3 squares	4 rows of 4 squares	5 rows of 5 squares	6 rows of 6 squares	
From each petal fabric	(5) 4½in (11.4cm) x WOF strips	(7) 4½in (11.4cm) x WOF strips	(9) 4½in (11.4cm) x WOF strips	(7) 4½in (11.4cm) x WOF strips	
	Subcut (36) Small template A	Subcut (48) Small template A	Subcut (60) Small template A	Subcut (48) Small template A	A
	and (12) Small template B	and (16) Small template B	and (20) Small template B	and (16) Small template B	B
Background fabrics	(3) 4½in (11.4cm) x WOF strips	(4) 4½in (11.4cm) x WOF strips	(4) 4½in (11.4cm) x WOF strips	(4) 4½in (11.4cm) x WOF strips	
	Subcut (36) Small template B	Subcut (48) Small template B	Subcut (60) Small template B	Subcut (48) Small template B	C
From each center fabric	(2) 4½in (11.4cm) x WOF strips	(2) 4½in (11.4cm) x WOF strips	(3) 4½in (11.4cm) x WOF strips	(3) 4½in (11.4cm) x WOF strips	
	Subcut (12) Small template A	Subcut (16) Small template A	Subcut (20) Small template A	Subcut (16) Small template A	D
Binding	(6) 2½in (6.4cm) x WOF strips	(7) 2½in (6.4cm) x WOF strips	(9) 2½in (6.4cm) x WOF strips	(10) 2½in (6.4cm) x WOF strips	

Hot tip

You will need three shades of the same color for each flower block. Decide on the placement of each shade—whether it will be center, petals, or background—before cutting.

Note
- Please read through all the instructions before beginning.
- Fabric quantities assume a WOF of 42in (107cm).
- All seams have a ¼in (6mm) seam allowance.

Cutting instructions

1. Cut all Small Template A, a combination of Small Template A and Small Template B, or all Template B on a strip as shown in the diagrams below. Each piece has a letter label in the cutting list that will help with organization and construction later. After cutting, sort all the pieces by color, then by letter.

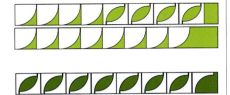

Drunkard's Path construction

2. Gather twelve A pieces, four B pieces, twelve C pieces and four D pieces in one color. Sew the pieces together in the combinations shown following the Drunkard's Path technique in "Quilting Essentials."

Flower block construction

3. Arrange the units as shown below. Place two units right sides together and sew the seam, then open out. Repeat until you have sewn three of the A/C units and one B/D unit together. Press the seam of the top row to the right and the bottom row to the left.

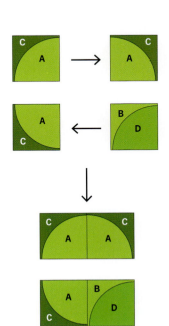

4. Place the rows right sides together, making sure the center seams align and are nested, then sew the seam. Press the seam towards the bottom.

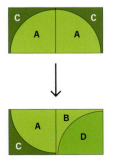

5. Repeat steps 3 and 4 to make a total of four petal units measuring 8½ x 8½in (21.6 x 21.6cm).

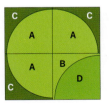

6 Arrange the four petal units so that the D pieces are all in the center. First sew the units together in two rows and press the seams open. Then sew the rows together to make a flower block measured 16½ x 16½in (42 x 42cm).

7 Repeat steps 2–6 to make the number of blocks in each color that you need for the size you are making:

Small	3 blocks in each of three colors
Medium	4 blocks in each of four colors
Large	5 blocks in each of five colors
Mega	4 blocks in each of nine colors

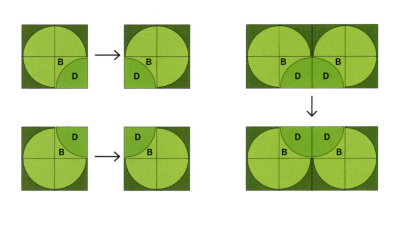

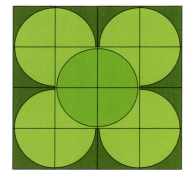

Quilt construction

8 Lay out the blocks in rows to the size you are making, following the layouts shown. Sew the blocks together to make the number of rows you need, then sew the rows together.

9 Iron the seams open or nest the seams, whatever technique is preferred.

10 When the quilt top is complete, refer to "Assembling your quilt" and choose your preferred methods to layer, quilt, and finish your quilt.

SMALL

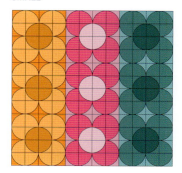

MEDIUM

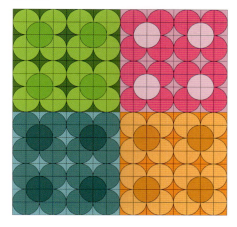

LARGE

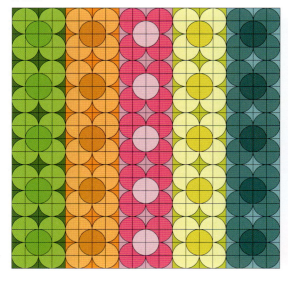

MEGA

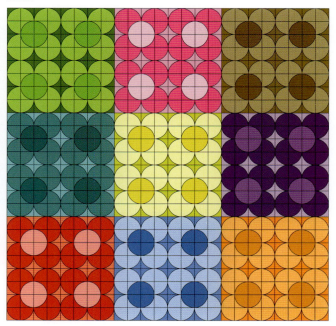

SKILL LEVEL
ADVANCED

Light My Fire

Comin' in hot! You may not want retro-style wallpaper in your home like me, but how about a quilt with that inspiration? Retro wallpaper makes such an impact and has a great vibe, and so will this quilt with its bold, block colors and repeating flame design.

Tools & Materials

- Rotary cutter
- Cutting mat
- Retro Blooms Small Template A and B (see Templates)
- Fabric shears (optional)
- Pins
- Fabric glue (if using the glue method for curves)
- Sewing machine
- Thread to match fabrics
- 6½ x 24in quilting ruler
- Stiletto or tweezers
- Metal straight edge
- Iron and ironing board
- Spray starch (optional)

Fabric requirements

	Small	Medium	Large	Mega
Finished size	56½in (143.5cm) square	71in (180.3cm) square	85in (215.9cm) square	99in (251.5cm) square
	8 blocks	13 blocks	18 blocks	25 blocks
Fabric 1 (red)	⅝ yard (57.2cm)	1 yard (91.4cm)	1¼ yards (114.3cm)	1¾ yards (160cm)
Fabric 2 (orange)	1 yard (91.4cm)	1½ yards (137.2cm)	2⅛ yards (194.3cm)	2⅞ yards (162.9cm)
Fabric 3 (yellow)	1¼ yards (114.3cm)	1⅞ yards (171.5cm)	2⅝ yards (240cm)	3¼ yards (297.2cm)
Fabric 4 (white)	1½ yards (137.2cm)	2 yards (182.9cm)	3 yards (274.3cm)	4⅛ yards (377.2cm)
Backing (with 4in/10cm overage)	3⅝ yards (331.5cm)	4⅓ yards (396.2cm)	6½ yards (594.4cm)	9 yards (823cm)
Batting/wadding (with 4in/10cm overage)	1⅞ yards, 90in wide (171.5cm, 228.6cm wide)	2⅛ yards, 90in wide (194.3cm, 228.6cm wide)	2⅝ yards, 108in wide (240cm, 274.3cm wide)	2¾ yards, 120in wide (251.5cm, 304.8cm wide)
Binding (2½in/6.4cm strips)	½ yard (45.7cm)	⅝ yard (57.2cm)	⅔ yard (61cm)	⅞ yard (80cm)

Note
- Please read through all the instructions before beginning.
- Fabric quantities assume a WOF of 42in (107cm).
- All seams have a ¼in (6mm) seam allowance.

Cutting instructions
1 Using a rotary cutter and cutting mat, cut all the pieces listed in the cutting table. Each piece has a letter label that identifies its size and color to help with organization and construction later.

Drunkard's Path construction
2 Gather all the A, C, D, G, H, and K pieces. Use the Drunkard's Path technique in "Quilting Essentials" to make up the number of units as shown for the size of quilt you are making:

    Small 16 of each
  Medium 26 of each
    Large 36 of each
    Mega 50 of each

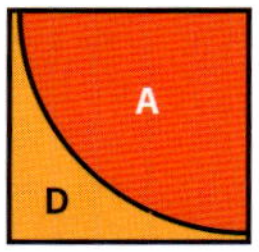

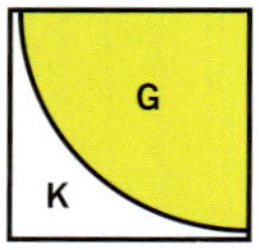

3 Trim the Drunkard's Path units to 4½in (11.5cm), then divide all the units into two equal piles and place half of the B pieces in a third pile.

4 Assemble the Drunkard's Path units and B pieces as shown below. Place the first two with right sides together and sew the seam. Press the seam toward the matching fabric each time. Add the next one in the same way until you have joined four in a row. Repeat until you have used all the Drunkard's Path units in the first pile.

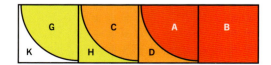

CUTTING	Small	Medium	Large	Mega	Piece
	8 blocks	13 blocks	18 blocks	25 blocks	
Fabric 1	(2) 4¾in (12cm) x WOF strips	(4) 4¾in (12cm) x WOF strips	(5) 4¾in (12cm) x WOF strips	(7) 4¾in (12cm) x WOF strips	
	Subcut (16) Small template A	Subcut (26) Small template A	Subcut (36) Small template A	Subcut (50) Small template A	A
	(2) 4½in (11.4cm) x WOF strips	(3) 4½in (11.4cm) x WOF strips	(4) 4½in (11.4cm) x WOF strips	(6) 4½in (11.4cm) x WOF strips	
	Subcut (16) 4½in (11.4cm) squares	Subcut (26) 4½in (11.4cm) squares	Subcut (36) 4½in (11.4cm) squares	Subcut (50) 4½in (11.4cm) squares	B
Fabric 2	(4) 4¾in (12cm) x WOF strips	(6) 4¾in (12cm) x WOF strips	(8) 4¾in (12cm) x WOF strips	(10) 4¾in (12cm) x WOF strips	
	Subcut (16) Small template A	Subcut (26) Small template A	Subcut (36) Small template A	Subcut (50) Small template A	C
	and (16) Small template B	and (26) Small template B	and (36) Small template B	and (50) Small template B	D
	(3) 4½in (11.4cm) x WOF strips	(5) 4½in (11.4cm) x WOF strips	(7) 4½in (11.4cm) x WOF strips	(10) 4½in (11.4cm) x WOF strips	
	Subcut (8) 4½ x 8½in (11.4 x 21.6cm)	Subcut (13) 4½ x 8½in (11.4 x 21.6cm)	Subcut (18) 4½ x 8½in (11.4 x 21.6cm)	Subcut (25) 4½ x 8½in (11.4 x 21.6cm)	E
	and (8) 4½in (11.4cm) squares	and (13) 4½in (11.4cm) squares	and (18) 4½in (11.4cm) squares	and (25) 4½in (11.4cm) squares	F
Fabric 3	(4) 4¾in (12cm) x WOF strips	(6) 4¾in (12cm) x WOF strips	(8) 4¾in (12cm) x WOF strips	(10) 4¾in (12cm) x WOF strips	
	Subcut (16) Small template A	Subcut (26) Small template A	Subcut (36) Small template A	Subcut (50) Small template A	G
	and (16) Small template B	and (26) Small template B	and (36) Small template B	and (50) Small template B	H
	(4) 4½in (11.4cm) x WOF strips	(7) 4½in (11.4cm) x WOF strips	(9) 4½in (11.4cm) x WOF strips	(13) 4½in (11.4cm) x WOF strips	
	Subcut (8) 4½ x 12½in (11.4 x 31.8cm)	Subcut (13) 4½ x 12½in (11.4 x 31.8cm)	Subcut (18) 4½ x 12½in (11.4 x 31.8cm)	Subcut (25) 4½ x 12½in (11.4 x 31.8cm)	I
	and (8) 4½ x 8½in (11.4 x 21.6cm)	and (13) 4½ x 8½in (11.4 x 21.6cm)	and (18) 4½ x 8½in (11.4 x 21.6cm)	and (25) 4½ x 8½in (11.4 x 21.6cm)	J
Fabric 4	(2) 4¾in (12cm) x WOF strips	(2) 4¾in (12cm) x WOF strips	(3) 4¾in (12cm) x WOF strips	(3) 4¾in (12cm) x WOF strips	
	Subcut (16) Small template B	Subcut (26) Small template B	Subcut (36) Small template B	Subcut (50) Small template B	K
	(9) 4½in (11.4cm) x WOF strips	(13) 4½in (11.4cm) x WOF strips	(19) 4½in (11.4cm) x WOF strips	(26) 4½in (11.4cm) x WOF strips	
	Sew 5 strips end to end	Sew 6 strips end to end	Sew 10 strips end to end	Sew 12 strips end to end	
	Subcut (1) 4½ x 86in (11.4 x 218.5cm)				L
	and (2) 4½ x 46½in (11.4 x 118.1cm)				M
		Subcut (1) 4½ x 108in (11.4 x 274.3cm)			P
		and (2) 4½ x 68in (11.4 x 172.8cm)			Q
			Subcut (1) 4½ x 122in (11.4 x 309.9cm)		S
			and (2) 4½ x 86in (11.4 x 218.5cm)		L
			and (2) 4½ x 46in (11.4 x 116.9cm)		M
				Subcut (1) 4½ x 142in (11.4 x 360.8cm)	T
				and (2) 4½ x 108in (11.4 x 274.3cm)	P
				and (2) 4½ x 68in (11.4 x 172.8cm)	Q
	From remaining WOF strips	From remaining WOF strips	From remaining WOF strips	From remaining WOF strips	
	Subcut (2) 4½ x 20in (11.4 x 51cm)		Subcut (2) 4½ x 20in (11.4 x 51cm)		N
	and (6) 4½ x 16½in (11.4 x 42cm)	Subcut (12) 4½ x 16½in (11.4 x 42cm)	and (16) 4½ x 16½in (11.5 x 42cm)	Subcut (24) 4½ x 16½in (11.5 x 42cm)	O
		and (2) 4½ x 26in (11.4 x 66cm)		and (2) 4½ x 26in (11.4 x 66cm)	R
Binding	(7) 2½in (6.4cm) x WOF strips	(8) 2½in (6.4cm) x WOF strips	(9) 2½in (6.4cm) x WOF strips	(11) 2½in (6.4cm) x WOF strips	

5 With the second pile you need to rotate all the Drunkard's Path units by 90 degrees. Sew them together as in step 4, this time without adding a B square at the end. Put these pieces aside for the moment.

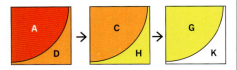

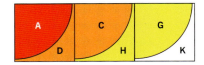

Log Cabin construction

6 Gather all the remaining B pieces and the E, F, I, and J pieces. Place a B and an F piece right sides together and sew the right-hand seam. Open out and press the seam open.

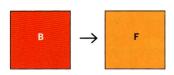

7 Place an E piece right sides together with the top edge aligned and sew together. Press the seam open.

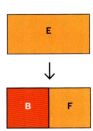

8 Next, add piece J as shown in the diagram below.

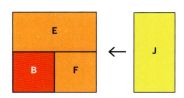

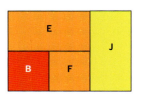

9 Finally add piece I along the top edge as shown.

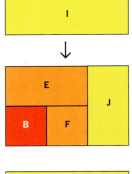

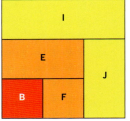

Block construction

10 Add the shorter Drunkard's Path strip along the bottom edge of the Log Cabin unit, making sure all the colors and seams match up.

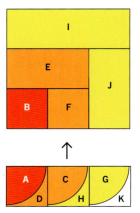

11 Finally add the longer Drunkard's Path unit on the left-hand side, again making sure the seams and colors match.

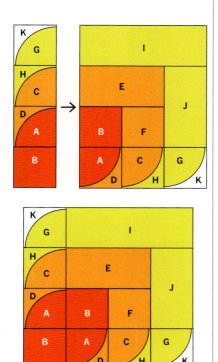

Quilt construction

12 You will need some half and quarter blocks to fill in at the edges, so make the following cuts for size of quilt you are making:

Small	2 vertical cuts and 2 horizontal cuts
Medium	2 vertical cuts, 2 horizontal cuts, and 1 quartered cut
Large	3 vertical cuts and 3 horizontal cuts
Mega	3 vertical cuts, 3 horizontal cuts, and 1 quartered cut

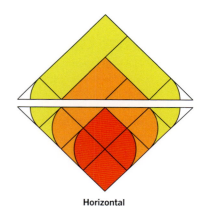

Horizontal

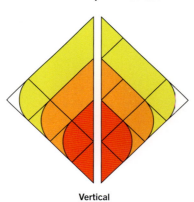

Vertical

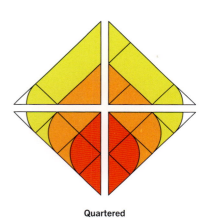

Quartered

13 Arrange the blocks, part blocks, and sashing strips according to the diagram for the size you are making.

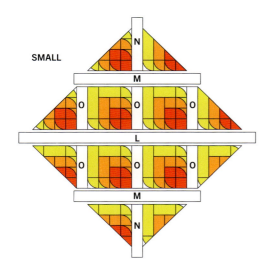

SMALL

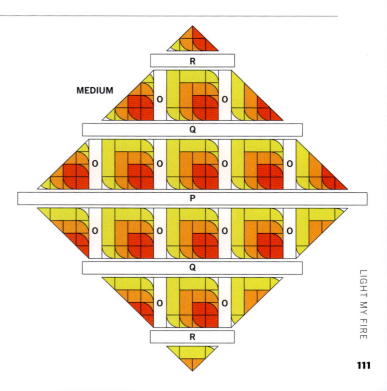

MEDIUM

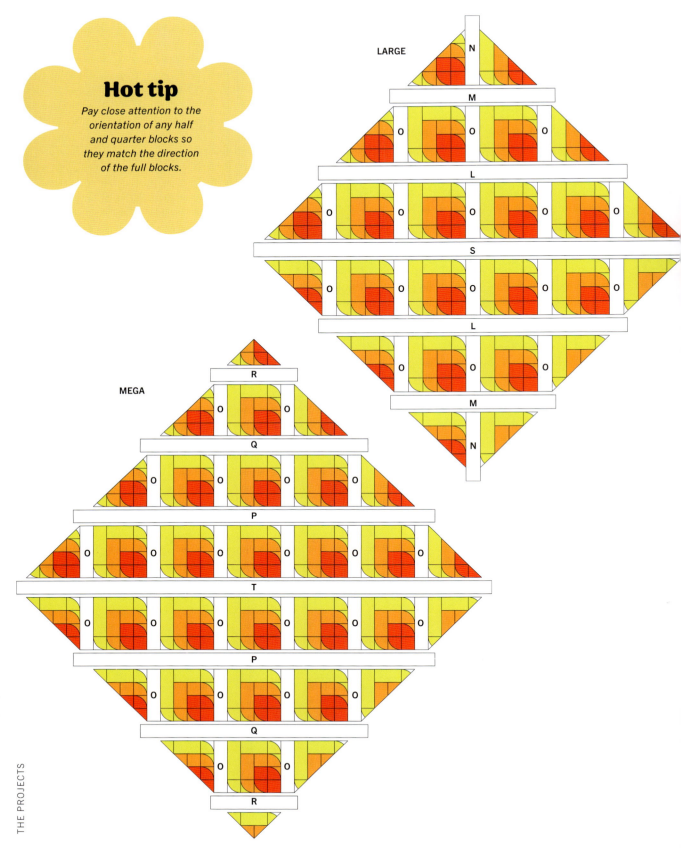

14 Sew the blocks and sashing together for the size you are making. Make sure that all the O sashing rows run in straight lines to get the full effect of the flame design.

15 Iron the seams open or nest the seams, whatever technique is preferred. Trim the extra sashing sticking out from edges of the quilt so it has straight edges all round.

16 When the quilt top is complete, refer to "Assembling your quilt" and choose your preferred methods to layer, quilt, and finish your quilt.

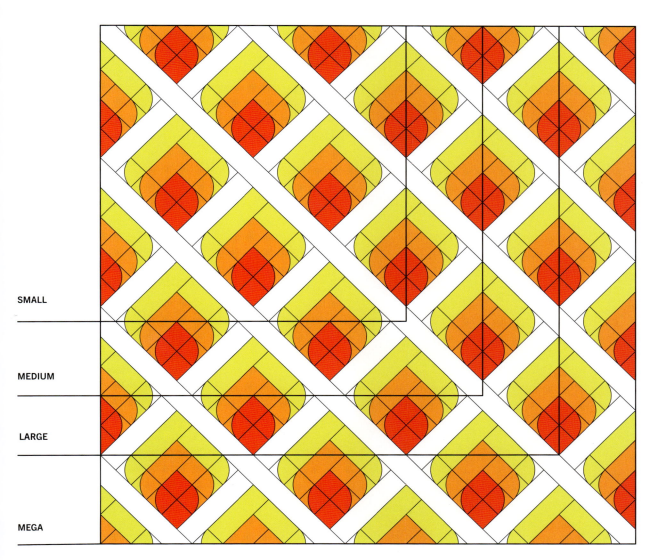

SMALL

MEDIUM

LARGE

MEGA

**SKILL LEVEL
ADVANCED**

Retro Blooms

When picturing the 1960s and '70s, I see a kaleidoscope of colors, so that was the basis for this flowery pattern. In the traditional version all the blocks are identical, but with the scrappy version Fabrics 1 and 2 are different in each block, and the snowball corners to the blocks are made with Fabric 1 instead of Fabric 4.

Tools & Materials

- 6½ x 24in quilting ruler
- Rotary cutter
- Cutting mat
- Retro Blooms Large Template A and B (see Templates)
- Retro Blooms Small Template A and B (see Templates)
- Pins
- Fabric glue (if using the glue method for curves)
- Sewing machine
- Thread to match fabrics
- Iron and ironing board
- Stiletto or tweezers
- Pinking shears (optional)
- Pillow form (if making a pillow)

Fabric requirements

	Pillow	Small	Medium	Large
Finished size	24in (61cm) square 1 block	48in (122cm) square 2 rows of 2 blocks	72in (182.9cm) square 3 rows of 3 blocks	96in (243.8cm) square 4 rows of 4 blocks
Traditional version				
Fabric 1 (corner quarter-circles)	(4) 7in (17.8cm) squares or (1) Fat quarter	¾ yard (68.6cm)	1¼ yards (114.3cm)	2¼ yards (205.7cm)
Fabric 2 (outer petals)	⅓ yard (30.5cm) or (1) Fat quarter	1 yard (91.4cm)	2⅛ yard (194.3cm)	3½ yard (320cm)
Scrappy version				
Fabric 1 (corner quarter-circles)	(1) Fat quarter	(4) Fat quarters	(9) Fat quarters	(16) Fat quarters
Fabric 2 (outer petals)	(1) Fat quarter	(4) Fat quarters	(9) Fat quarters	(16) Fat quarters
Both versions				
Fabric 3 (inner petals)	¼ yard (23cm) or (1) Fat quarter	⅝ yard (57.2cm)	1⅜ yards (125.7cm)	2½ yards (228.6cm)
Fabric 4 (flower center)	(1) 8½in (21.6cm) square (4) 2in (5cm) squares	⅓ yard (30.5cm)	1 yard (91.4cm)	1⅛ yards (102.9cm)
Background	⅜ yard (34.3cm) or (1) Fat quarter	1⅛ yards (102.9cm)	2¼ yards (205.7cm)	4 yards (365.8cm)
Backing (with 4in/10cm overage)	⅞ yard (80cm)	2⅓ yards (213.4cm)	4½ yards (411.5cm)	8⅔ yards (792.5cm)
Batting/wadding (with 4in/10cm overage)	¾ yard (68.6cm)	1⅝ yard, 60in wide (148.6cm, 152.4cm wide)	2¼ yards, 90in wide (205.7cm, 228.6cm wide)	3 yards, 120in wide (274.3cm, 304.8cm wide)
Binding (2½in/6.4cm strips)	¼ yard (23cm)	½ yard (45.7cm)	⅝ yard (57.2cm)	¾ yard (68.6cm)
Pillow back	¾ yard (68.6cm)			

Note

- Please read through all the instructions before beginning.
- Fabric quantities assume a WOF of 42in (107cm).
- All seams have a ¼in (6mm) seam allowance.

Cutting instructions

1 For each block, follow the cutting list and also refer to the cutting diagrams. The cutting list gives a letter label to each piece to help with organization and construction later on.

FAT QUARTER CUTTING DIAGRAMS

Fabric 1

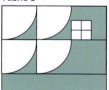

Large template A

Fabric 2

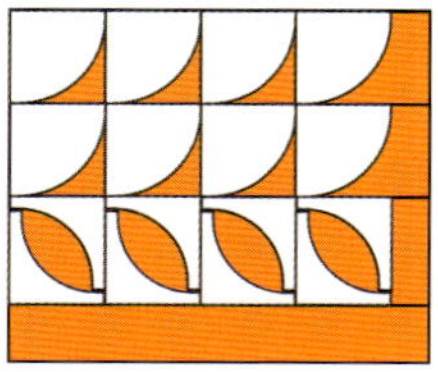

Small template A & B

YARDAGE CUTTING DIAGRAMS
Background

Large and small template B

Fabric 2

Small template A & B

Cutting

	Pillow	Small	Medium	Large	Piece label
Traditional version					
Fabric 1	(4) 7in (17.8cm) squares	(3) 7in (17.8cm) x WOF strips	(6) 7 n (17.8cm) x WOF strips	(11) 7in (17.8cm) x WOF strips	
	Subcut (4) Large Template A	Subcut (16) Large Template A	Subcut (36) Large Template A	Subcut (64) Large Template A	A
Fabric 2	(2) 4¾in (12cm) x WOF strips	(7) 4¾in (12cm) x WOF strips	(15) 4¾in (12cm) x WOF strips	(26) 4¾in (12cm) x WOF strips	
	Subcut (8) Small Template A	Subcut (32) Small Template A	Subcut (72) Small Template A	Subcut (128) Small Template A	B
	and (8) Small Template B	and (32) Small Template B	and (72) Small Template B	and (128) Small Template B	C
Fabric 4		(1) 8½in (21.6cm) x WOF strip	(3) 8½in (21.6cm) x WOF strips	(4) 8½in (21.6cm) x WOF strips	
	(1) 8½in (21.6cm) square	Subcut (4) 8½in (21.6cm) squares	Subcut (9) 8½in (21.6cm) squares	Subcut (16) 8½in (21.6cm) squares	F
	(4) 2in (5cm) squares	and (16) 2in (5cm) squares	and (36) 2in (5cm) squares	and (64) 2in (5cm) squares	G
Scrappy version					
Fabric 1	Per fat quarter:	Per fat quarter:	Per fat quarter:	Per fat quarter:	
See cutting diagram		(7) 7in (17.8cm) x WOFQ strips	(2) 7in (17.8cm) x WOFQ strips	(2) 7in (17.8cm) x WOFQ strips	
	(4) Large Template A	Subcut (4) Large Template A	Subcut (4) Large Template A	Subcut (4) Large Template A	A
	(4) 2in (5cm) squares	and (4) 2in (5cm) squares	and (4) 2in (5cm) squares	and (4) 2in (5cm) squares	J
Fabric 2	Per fat quarter:	Per fat quarter:	Per fat quarter:	Per fat quarter:	
See cutting diagram		(3) 4¾in (12cm) x WOFQ strips	(3) 4¾in (12cm) x WOFQ strips	(3) 4¾in (12cm) x WOFQ strips	
	(8) Small Template A	Subcut (8) Small Template A	Subcut (8) Small Template A	Subcut (8) Small Template A	B
	(8) Small Template B	and (8) Small Template B	and (8) Small Template B	and (8) Small Template B	C
Fabric 4		(1) 8½in (21.6cm) x WOF strip	(3) 8½in (21.6cm) x WOF strips	(4) 8½in (21.6cm) x WOF strips	
	(1) 8½in (21.6cm) square	Subcut (4) 8½in (21.6cm) squares	Subcut (9) 8½in (21.6cm) squares	Subcut (16) 8½in (21.6cm) squares	F
Both versions					
Fabric 3	(1) 4¾in (12cm) x WOF strip	(4) 4¾in (12cm) x WOF strips	(9) 4¾in (12cm) x WOFQ strips	(16) 4¾in (12cm) x WOFQ strips	
	OR (2) 4¾in (12cm) x WOFQ strips				
	Subcut (8) Small Template A	Subcut (32) Small Template A	Subcut (72) Small Template A	Subcut (128) Small Template A	D
	(1) 2in (5cm) x WOF strip				
	OR (1) 2in (5cm) x WOFQ strip	(1) 2in (5cm) x WOF strip	(2) 2in (5cm) x WOF strips	(4) 2in (5cm) x WOF strips	
	Subcut (4) 2in (5cm) squares	Subcut (16) 2in (5cm) squares	Subcut (36) 2in (5cm) squares	Subcut (64) 2in (5cm) squares	E
Background	(1) 8¾in (22.2cm) x WOF strip	(4) 8¾in (22.2cm) x WOF strips	(9) 8¾in (22.2cm) x WOF strips	(16) 8¾in (22.2cm) x WOF strips	
See cutting diagram	Subcut (4) Large Template B	Subcut (16) Large Template B	Subcut (36) Large Template B	Subcut (64) Large Template B	H
	and (8) Small Template B	and (32) Small Template B	and (72) Small Template B	and (128) Small Template B	I
Pillow backing	26½in (67.3cm)				
Binding		(6) 2½in (6.4cm) strips	(8) 2½in (6.4cm) strips	(10) 2½in (6.4cm) strips	
Pillow back	(2) 15½ x 25in (39.4 x 63.5cm) strips				

The diagram below shows what you will need for one full Retro Blooms block. Note that in the Scrappy version piece G is piece J instead.

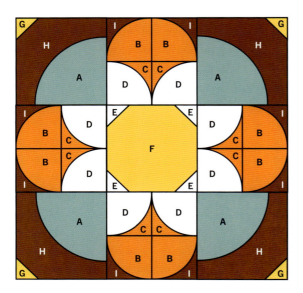

Hot tip

If you are making the Traditional Version, you will cut your four 2in (5cm) squares from Fabric 4 instead of Fabric 1.

Snowball corner construction

2. Draw a diagonal line, corner to corner, on the wrong side of all E and G or E and J squares (depending on whether you are making the Traditional or Scrappy version). These corners will be used on the center unit and on the four large Drunkard's Path units for the four corners. The method is the same for both versions.

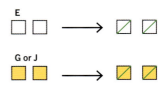

3. Place a center square F with right side facing up and add an E square right sides together over each corner. Pin in place making sure that the diagonal line goes across the corner.

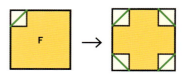

4. Sew along the drawn line on each corner. Trim each seam allowance down to ¼in (6mm) as indicated by the red line on the diagram below. Open out the corner and press the seams open.

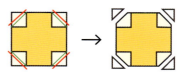

5 This completes the center unit. Repeat steps 3 and 4 as many times as needed to make a center unit for the size you are making—you will need:

Pillow 1
Small 4
Medium 9
Large 16

Large Drunkard's Path construction

6 For each corner Drunkard's Path you will need four A—in the same fabric if you are making the Scrappy version—and four H. Make these pieces up into four identical units following the instructions for Drunkard's Path in the Quilting Essentials chapter.

7 Trim each unit to 8½ x 8½in (21.6 x 21.6cm) by trimming along the edges of section H as shown below.

8 Using the method in steps 2–3, add a snowball corner to one corner, using G pieces for the Traditional version and J pieces for the Scrappy, and the same method as for the center unit. This completes the four corner units for one block.

9 Repeat steps 6–8 as many times as needed to make the number of corner units for the size you are making—you will need:

Pillow 4
Small 16
Medium 36
Large 64

Small Drunkard's Path construction

10 For the four Drunkard's Path "petals" on each block you will need eight B pieces—in the same fabric if you are making the Scrappy version—eight I pieces, eight D pieces, and eight C pieces. Make these pieces up into eight identical units in each colorway following the instructions for Drunkard's Path.

11 Arrange the colorways in pairs as shown below, then place each set right sides together and sew the center seam. Open out and press the seam open.

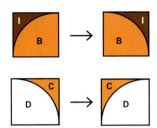

12 Arrange the sets as shown below, then place right sides together and sew the center seam. Open out and press the seam open. This creates one petal unit.

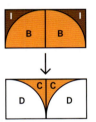

13 Repeat steps 10–12 as many times as needed to make the number of petal units for the size you are making—you will need:

Pillow 4
Small 16
Medium 36
Large 64

Retro Bloom block construction

14 Arrange a set of units in three rows of three as shown below. Sew the units together in rows. Press seams open.

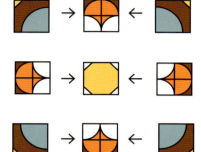

15 Sew the rows together.

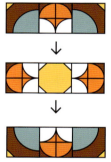

16 Press the completed block. Each block should measure 24½ x 24½in (62.3 x 62.3cm). Repeat steps 14 and 15 to make the number of blocks for the size you are making. You will need:

Pillow	1
Small	4
Medium	9
Large	16

Pillow construction

17 When the pillow top is complete, layer the top, batting, and backing and quilt using your preferred methods.

18 Follow the Envelope Pillow Back instructions in the Quilting Essentials chapter to complete your pillow.

Quilt construction

19 Assemble the blocks into the number of rows you need for the version you are making—if you have made the Scrappy version, lay all the blocks out and move them around until you have a pleasing arrangement.

20 Join the rows together, alternately pressing the seams on each row to right and left. Sew the rows together, nesting the previous seams and then press the seam just made open.

21 Refer to "Assembling your quilt" and choose your preferred methods to layer, quilt, and finish your piece.

SCRAPPY
VERSION

Pillow

Small

Medium

Mega

TRADITIONAL
VERSION

Pillow

Small

Medium

Mega

SKILL LEVEL
ADVANCED

High Fidelity

My ode to the music of the 1970s, High Fidelity. This quilt was inspired specifically by the recording equipment and music technology of the time, because it was the music of this decade that really made it special. So, this quilt is to show my love for it all.

Tools & Materials

- Rotary cutter
- Cutting mat
- High Fidelity Templates A, B, C, and D (see Templates)
- Fabric glue (if using the glue method for curves)
- Pins
- Sewing machine
- Thread to match fabrics
- 6½ x 24in quilting ruler
- Metal straight edge
- Iron and ironing board
- Pinking shears (optional)
- Approx 14in (35.5cm) wooden dowel (if making wall hanging)

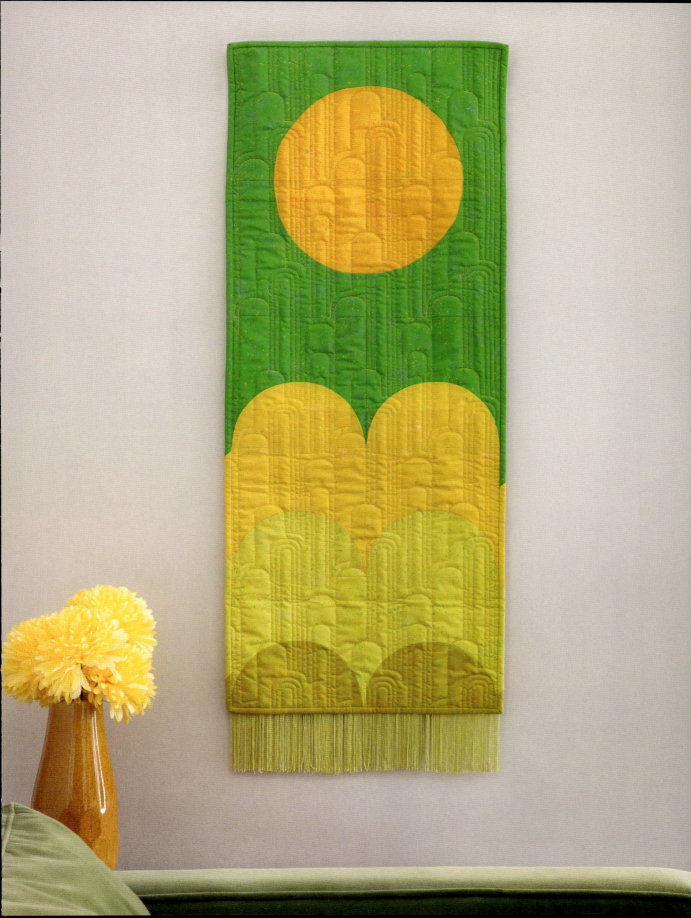

Fabric requirements

	Wall Hanging	Small	Medium	Large
Finished size	15 x 37½in (38.1 x 95.3cm)	45 x 52½in (114.3 x 133.3cm)	60 x 82½in (152.4 x 209.6cm)	75 x 82½in (190.5 x 209.6cm)
	1 circle block, 1 column, 5 colors	3 circle blocks, 3 columns, 7 colors	4 circle blocks, 4 columns, 7 colors	5 circle blocks, 5 columns, 7 colors
Fabric 1	⅝ yard (57.2cm)	2 yards (182.9cm)	2½ yards (228.6cm)	2⅝ yards (240cm)
Fabric 2	¼ yard (22.9cm)	⅜ yard (34.3cm)	½ yard (45.7cm)	¾ yard (68.6cm)
Fabric 3	⅓ yard (30.5cm)	⅝ yard (57.2cm)	¾ yard (68.6cm)	¾ yard (68.6cm)
Fabric 4	⅓ yard (30.5cm)	⅓ yard (30.5cm)	¾ yard (68.6cm)	¾ yard (68.6cm)
Fabric 5	⅓ yard (30.5cm)	⅓ yard (30.5cm)	¾ yard (68.6cm)	¾ yard (68.6cm)
Fabric 6		⅓ yard (30.5cm)	¾ yard (68.6cm)	¾ yard (68.6cm)
Fabric 7		¼ yard (22.9cm)	1⅜ yards (125.7cm)	1⅜ yards (125.7cm)
Backing (with 4in/10cm overage)	1¼ yards (114.3cm)	3 yards (274.3cm)	5⅔ yards (518.2cm)	5¾ yards (525.8cm)
Batting/wadding (with 4in/10cm overage)	⅝ yard, 60in wide (57.2cm, 152.4cm wide)	1½ yards, 60in wide (137.2cm, 152.4cm wide)	2 yards, 90in wide (182.9cm, 228.6cm wide)	2⅓ yards, 90in wide (213.4cm, 228.6cm wide)
Binding (2½in/6.4cm strips)	⅓ yard (30.5cm)	½ yard (45.7cm)	⅝ yard (57.2cm)	⅔ yard (61cm)

Note
- Please read through all the instructions before beginning.
- Fabric quantities assume a WOF of 42in (107cm).
- All seams have a ¼in (6mm) seam allowance.

Cutting instructions

1. The wall hanging uses five different fabrics, while the other projects all use seven. Follow the cutting guide carefully to make sure you cut the correct number of each piece from the correct colors. The cutting list also gives a letter label to each piece to help with organization and construction later.

Fabric 1
Fabric 2
Fabric 3
Fabric 4
Fabric 5
Fabric 6
Fabric 7

There are also four different templates—a small set for columns (A and B) and a large set for circle units (C and D). Note the half-circle templates need to have one edge placed on a fold for cutting to obtain a complete half-circle.

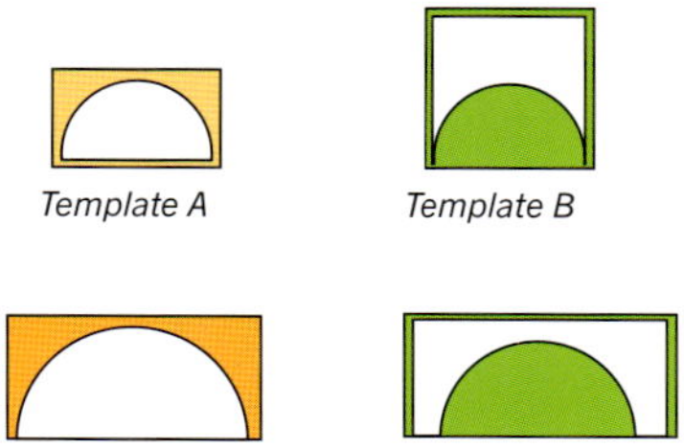

Template A   Template B

Template C   Template D

The quilts also have plain rectangles that are cut from Fabric 1—see the layout diagrams.

Circle block construction

2. Make the Circle blocks by making two halves for each using pieces D and C and the Half-circle technique from "Quilting Essentials." You will need the following halves for each project:

Wall hanging   2
Small   6
Medium   8
Large   10

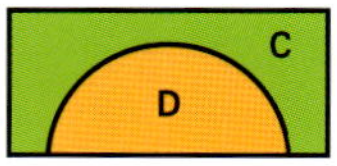

3. Sew two half-circle units together as shown below. Each circle block should measure 15½ x 15½in (39.4 x 39.4cm). You will need the following circle blocks for each project:

Wall hanging   1
Small   3
Medium   4
Large   5

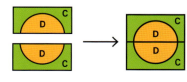

Cutting

Templates C and D need to have one edge placed to a fold when cutting to obtain a half-circle.

	Wall Hanging	Small	Medium	Large	Piece label
Fabric 1	(2) 8½in (21.6cm) x WOF	(2) 15½in (39.4cm) x WOF strips	(2) 15½in (39.4cm) x WOF strips	(3) 15½in (39.4cm) x WOF strips	
		Subcut (1) 15½ x 31½in (39.4 x 80cm) rectangle	Subcut (1) 15½ x 31½in (39.4 x 80cm) rectangle	Subcut (2) 15½ x 31½in (39.4 x 80cm) rectangles	A
		and (1) 15½ x 15½in (39.4 x 39.4cm) square	and (1) 15½ x 15½in (39.4 x 39.4cm) square	and (1) 15½ x 15½in (39.4 x 39.4cm) square	B
				and (2) Template D	C
	Subcut (2) Template D				C
	and (2) Template B				E
		(4) 8½in (21.6cm) x WOF strips	(6) 8½in (21.6cm) x WOF strips	(2) 8½in (21.6cm) x WOF strips	
		Subcut (6) Template B	Subcut (8) Template B	Subcut (10) Template B	E
		and (6) Template D	and (8) Template D		C
Fabric 2	(1) 5½in (14cm) x WOF strip	(2) 5½in (14cm) x WOF strips	(3) 5½in (14cm) x WOF strips	(4) 5½in (14cm) x WOF strips	
	Subcut (2) Template C	Subcut (6) Template C	Subcut (8) Template C	Subcut (10) Template C	D
Fabric 3	(1) 8½in (21.6cm) x WOF strip	(2) 8½in (21.6cm) x WOF strips	(2) 8½in (21.6cm) x WOF strips	(3) 8½in (21.6cm) x WOF strips	
	Subcut (2) Template B	Subcut (4) Template B	Subcut (8) Template B	Subcut (10) Template B	G
	and (2) Template A	and (6) Template A			F
			(2) 4½in (11.4cm) x WOF strips	(2) 4½in (11.4cm) x WOF strip	
			Subcut (8) Template A	Subcut (10) Template A	F
Fabric 4	(1) 8½in (21.6cm) x WOF strip	(1) 8½in (21.6cm) x WOF strip	(2) 8½in (21.6cm) x WOF strips	(3) 8½in (21.6cm) x WOF strips	
	Subcut (2) Template B	Subcut (2) Template B	Subcut (8) Template B	Subcut (10) Template B	H
	and (2) Template A				I
			(2) 4½in (11.4cm) x WOF strips	(2) 4½in (11.4cm) x WOF strips	
		and (4) Template A	Subcut (8) Template A	Subcut (10) Template A	I
Fabric 5	(1) 4¼in (10.8cm) x WOF strip	(1) 8½in (21.6cm) x WOF strip	(2) 8½in (21.6cm) x WOF strips	(3) 8½in (21.6cm) x WOF strips	
		Subcut (2) Template B	Subcut (8) Template B	Subcut (10) Template B	K
	Subcut (2) Template A	and (2) Template A			J
			(2) 4½in (11.4cm) x WOF strips	(2) 4½in (11.4cm) x WOF strips	
			Subcut (8) Template A	Subcut (10) Template A	J
Fabric 6		8½in (21.6cm) x WOF strip	(2) 8½in (21.6cm) x WOF strips	(3) 8½in (21.6cm) x WOF strips	
		Subcut (2) Template B	Subcut (8) Template B	Subcut (10) Template B	M
		and (2) Template A			L
			(2) 4½in (11.4cm) x WOF strips	(2) 4½in (11.4cm) x WOF strip	
			Subcut (8) Template A	Subcut (10) Template A	L
Fabric 7		(1) 4¼in (10.8cm) x WOF strip	(3) 15½in (39.4cm) x WOF strips	(3) 15½in (39.4cm) x WOF strips	
			Subcut (2) 15½ x 31½in (39.4 x 80cm) rectangles	Subcut (2) 15½ x 31½in (39.4 x 80cm) rectangles	O
			and (1) 15½ x 15½in (39.4 x 39.4cm) square	and (1) 15½ x 15½in (39.4 x 39.4cm) square	P
		Subcut (2) Template A	and (4) Template A	and (2) Template A	N
Backing	(2) 3½in (8.9cm) squares (for wall hanging corners)				
Binding	(4) 2½in (6.4cm) strips	(6) 2½in (6.4cm) strips	(8) 2½in (6.4cm) strips	(9) 2½in (6.4cm) strips	

Column block construction

4 Begin the column blocks by making units using the Half-circle technique in the Quilting Essentials chapter. See the table for how many units to make for each project. Trim each finished block to 8 x 8in (20.3 x 20.3cm).

	E/F	G/H	I/J	K/L	M/N
Wall hanging	2	2	2		
Small	6	4	4	2	2
Medium	8	8	8	8	8
Large	10	10	10	10	10

UNIT COMBINATIONS

5 Sew two matching column units together to make the column blocks by placing each pair right sides together to sew. Open out and press the seam to alternate sides. See the table for how many blocks to make for each project. Trim each finished block to 15½ x 8in (39.4 x 20.3cm).

	E/F	G/H	I/J	K/L	M/N
Wall hanging	1	1	1		
Small	3	2	2	1	1
Medium	4	4	4	4	4
Large	5	5	5	5	5

UNIT COMBINATIONS

Quilt construction

6 To assemble the project, follow the diagrams for the size you are making. First join the column blocks by placing each pair right sides together with the following pair to sew. Open out and press the seam to alternate sides to avoid bulky seams in one place. Add a circle block or a plain rectangle to the top of the relevant column, following the layout diagrams as a guide.

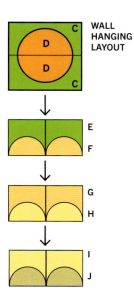

7 Sew the columns together in the same way, again following the layout diagrams.

8 If you are making a wall hanging, see "Making a wall hanging" for instructions on adding hanging corners. If you are not making a wall hanging, choose your preferred methods to layer, quilt and finish your piece.

MEDIUM LAYOUT

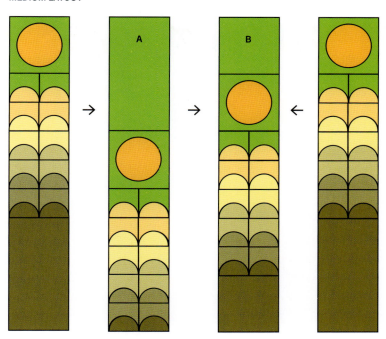

LARGE LAYOUT

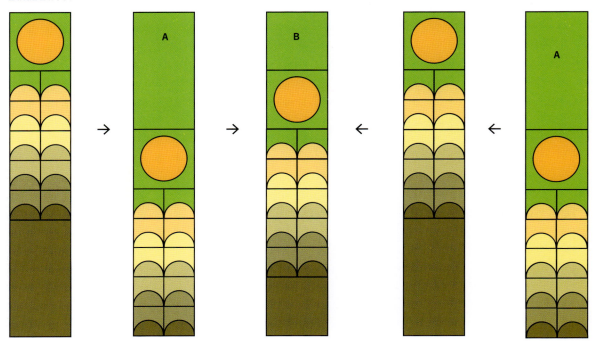

Templates

Here are all the templates you need to make the projects in this book. Refer to "Tools and materials" for information on how to size and use them. A printable PDF can also be found at www.bookmarkedhub.com.

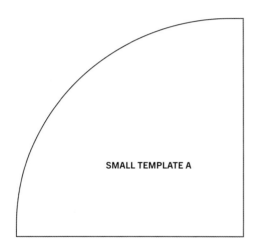

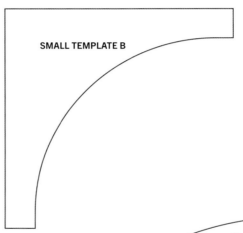

Templates at 50%

Retro Blooms: (4) Templates
- **Small Template A** = 4.8 x 4.8in (12.5 x 12.5cm)
- **Small Template B** = 4.8 x 4.8in (12.5 x 12.5cm)
- **Large Template A** = 6.8 x 6.8in (17.3 x 17.3cm)
- **Large Template B** = 8.7 x 8.7in (22.1 x 22.1cm)

(*Small Template A & B are used in* **Quilt 54** *and* **Light My Fire**)

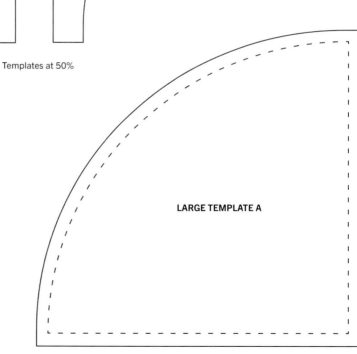

Template at 50%

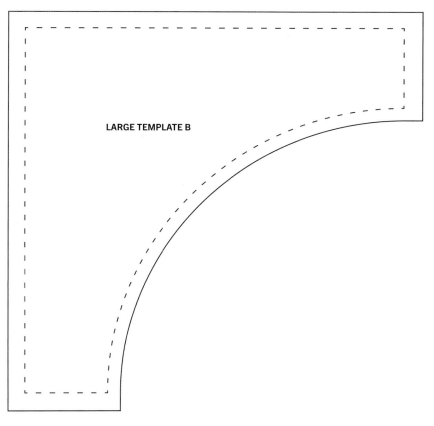

Template at 50%

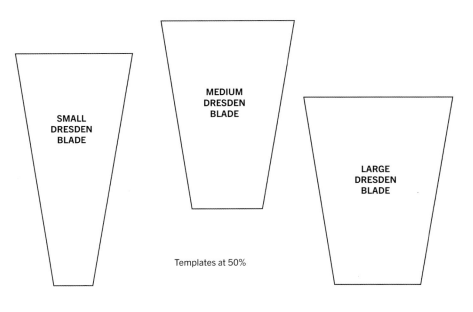

Templates at 50%

Stevie Pillow:

(9) Templates

- **Small Dresden Blade** = 2.5 x 5in (6.2 x 12.7cm)
- **Medium Dresden Blade** = 2.8 x 4in (7.1 x 10.2cm)
- **Large Dresden Blade** = 3.1 x 4in (7.9 x 10.2cm)

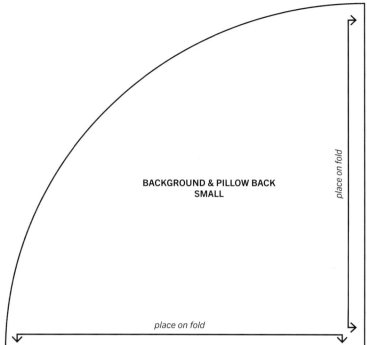

Stevie Pillow:
- **Mega Dresden Blade** = 3.4 x 4in (8.6 x 10.2cm)
- **Dresden Center** = 3.5 x 3.5in (8.9 x 8.9cm)
- **Background & Pillow Back** = SMALL, MEDIUM, LARGE, MEGA *(Small Dresden Blade & Dresden Center are used in **Op Art**)*

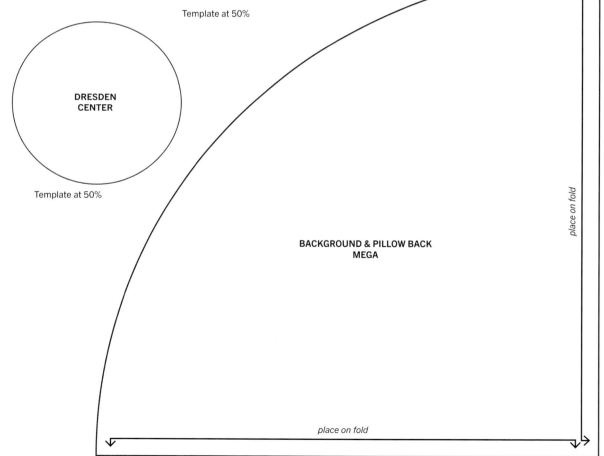

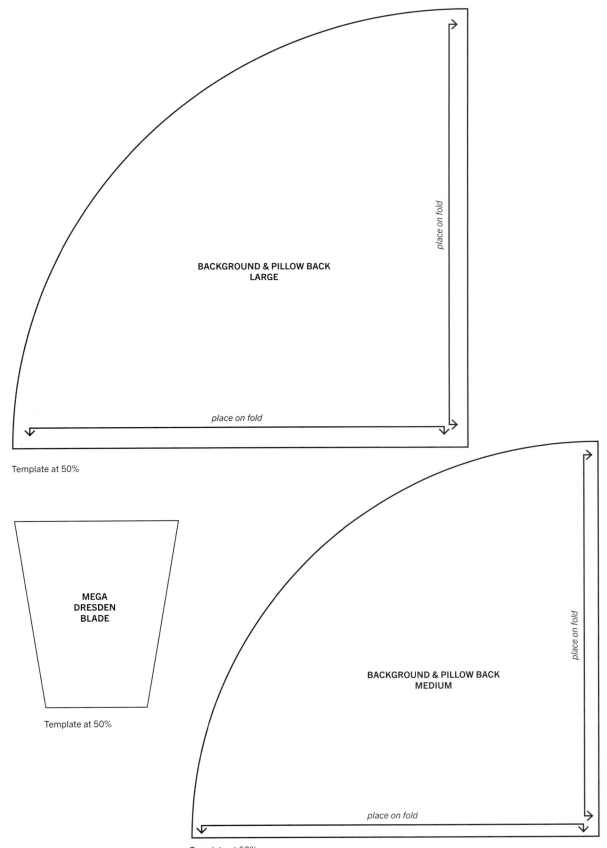

Trippy Dippy: (2) Templates
- **Template A** = 5.1 x 9.5in (13 x 24.1cm)
- **Template B** = 5.3 x 9.8in (13.5 x 24.8cm)

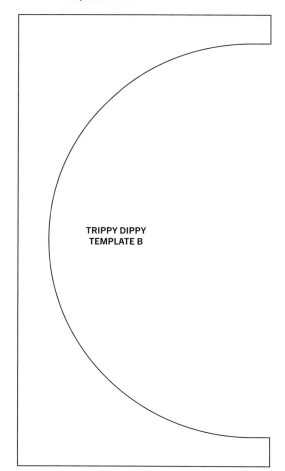

Template at 50%

TRIPPY DIPPY TEMPLATE A

Template at 50%

TRIPPY DIPPY TEMPLATE B

Patio Lanterns: (2) Templates
- **Triangle Template** = 2 x 6.8in (5.1 x 17.2cm)
- **Lantern Template** = 4.9 x 6in (12.4 x 15.3cm)

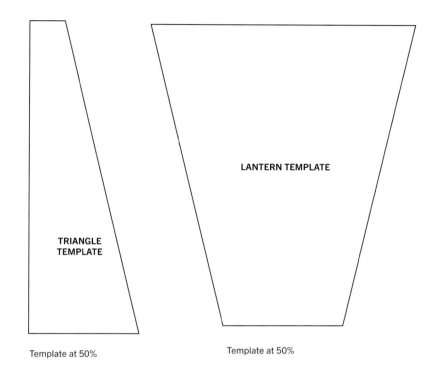

Flower Power: (2) Templates
- **Flower Power Template** = 15.5 x 15.8in (39.4 x 40.1cm)
- **Flower Power Center** = 3.1 x 2.5in (7.9 x 6.4cm)

Template at 25%

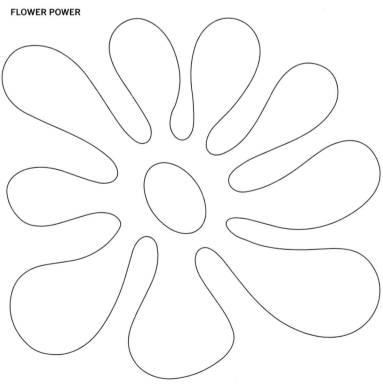

Template at 25%

High Fidelity: (4) Templates
- **A** = 8 x 4.3in (20 x 11cm)
- **B** = 8.5 x 8.3in (21.5 x 21cm)
- **C** = 10.5 x 5.8in (27 x 14.5cm)
- **D** = 15.5 x 8in (39 x 20.3cm)

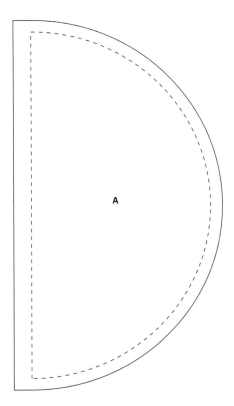

Templates at 50%

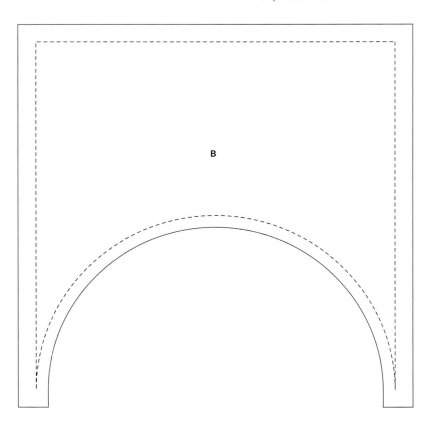

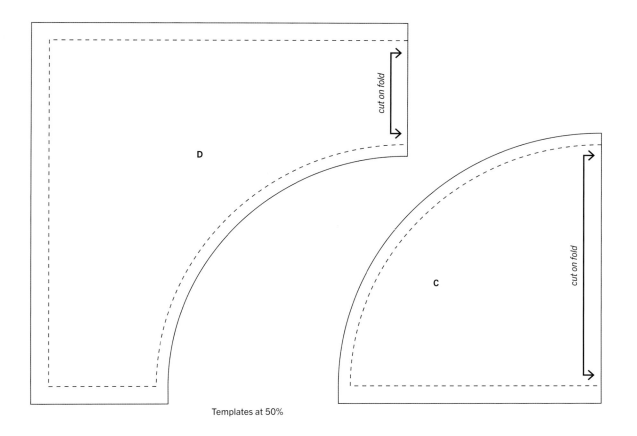

Templates at 50%

Outta Sight: (1) Template
- **Circle template** = 7.5 x 7.5in (19 x 19cm)

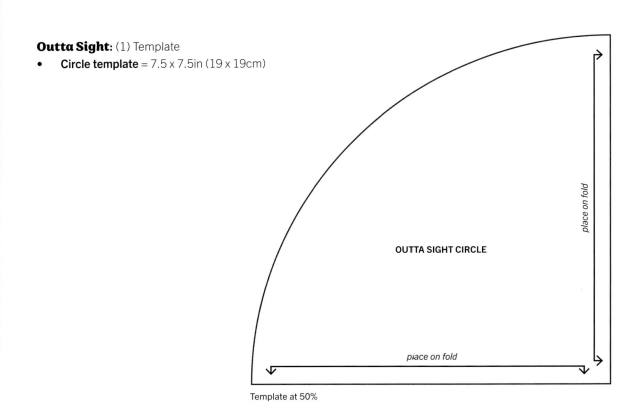

Template at 50%

Checkered Adventure + Appliqué

Adventure: (15) Templates
- **Flower 1A** = 19.1 x 19.1in (48.5 x 48.5cm)
- **Flower 2A** = 17.4 x 18.2in (44.2 x 46.2cm)
- **Flower 2D** = 8.3 x 8.7in (21.1 x 22.1cm)
- **Flower 3B** = 16.6 x 16.6in (42.2 x 42.2cm)
- **Flower 3D** = 8.7 x 8.7in (22.1 x 22.1cm)
- **Star 2B** = 13.2 x 15.6in (33.5 x 39.6cm)
- **Star 2D** = 8.2 x 9.7in (20.8 x 24.6cm)

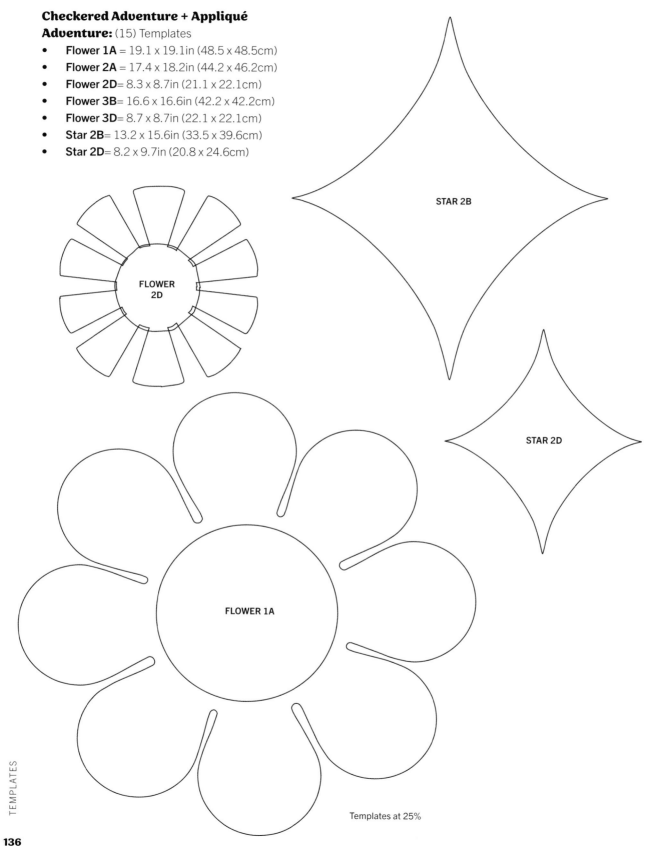

Templates at 25%

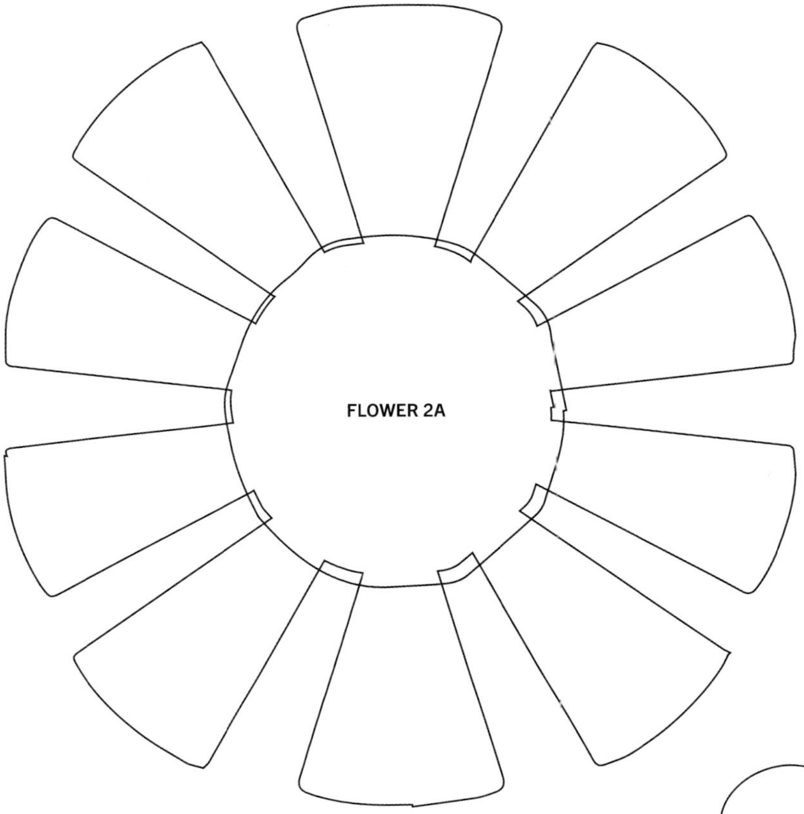

FLOWER 2A

Templates at 25%

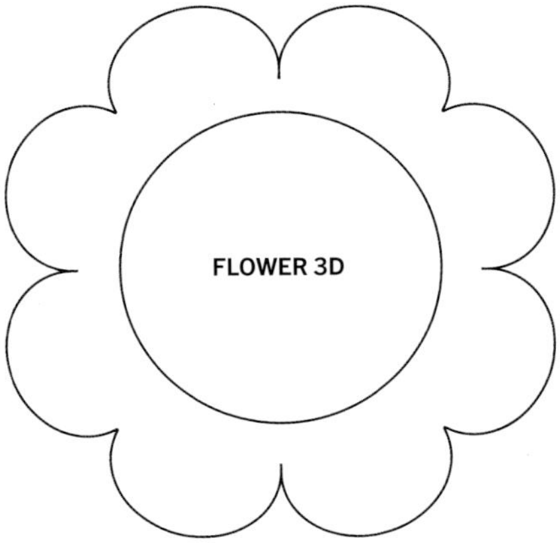

FLOWER 3D

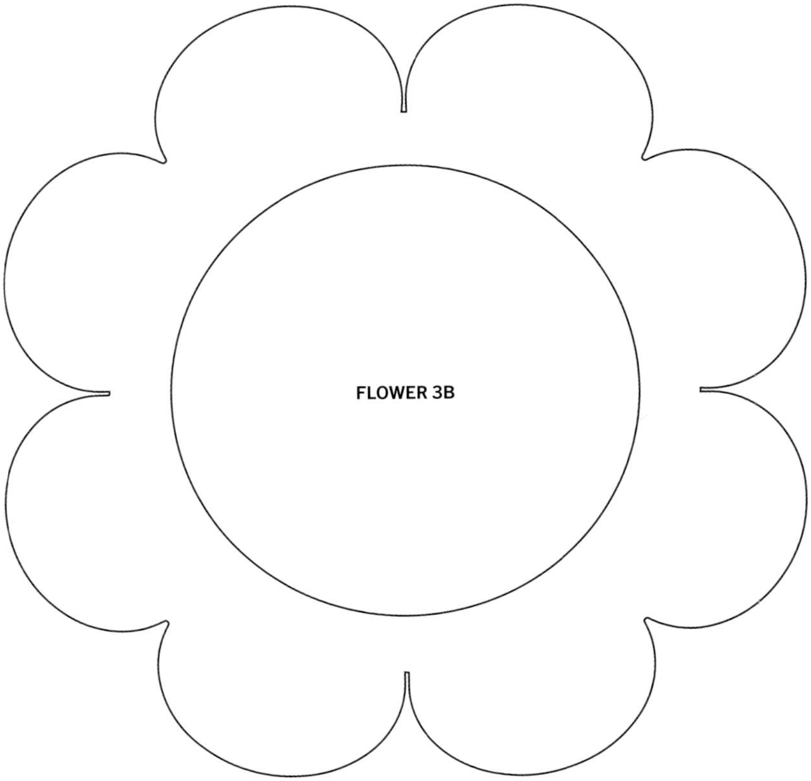

FLOWER 3B

TEMPLATES

137

STAR 1C

STAR 2A

Templates at 25%

MUSHROOM 1A

Checkered Adventure + Appliqué Adventure:
- **Mushroom 1A** = 19.3 x 19.4in (48.9 x 49.3cm)
- **Mushroom 1C** = 11.6 x 12.9in (29.5 x 32.8cm)
- **Mushroom 2C** = 13 x 13.1in (33 x 33.3cm)
- **Star 1A** = 18.4 x 17.4in (46.7 x 42.2cm)
- **Star 1C** = 12.8 x 13.5in (32.5 x 34.3cm)
- **Star 1D** = 8.9 x 8.4in (22.6 x 21.3cm)
- **Star 2A** = 16.5 x 19.6in (41.9 x 49.8cm)
- **Flower 1C** = 12.8 x 12.8in (32.4 x 32.4cm)

Glossary

Batting (Wadding)
The fluffy insulating material between the quilt top and quilt backing. This middle layer adds warmth and dimensionality to the quilt.

Chain piecing
Sewing blocks (or pieces of blocks) one after the other in a continuous chain without stopping or cutting the thread.

Directional fabrics
Fabrics that have a distinct nap or top and bottom to the design of fabric print.

Dresden plate block
A patchwork block made up of radiating blades that complete a circle. Named for Dresden porcelain plates popular during the Victorian era.

Drunkard's Path block
A patchwork block made up of quarter-circles sewn into squares that can give the illusion of staggered walking.

Fat quarter
A cut piece of fabric measuring 21 x 18in (55 x 45cm) in the US and 50 x 56cm (19 x 22in) in the UK.

Fusible turned edge appliqué
An appliqué technique that uses fusible interfacing sewn to the fabric, then turned so the raw edges of fabric are concealed.

Fusible web
Heat activated adhesive, often paper-backed, that bonds fabrics together.

Fussy cutting
Cutting a particular part of the fabric design (such as a shape or motif) to highlight a specific detail.

LOFQ
Length of fat quarter.

Log cabin block
A patchwork block of rectangles sewn around a square, which imitates the stacked logs of a log cabin.

Nesting
Aligning two seams so that the bulk of the fabrics line up, since they are pressed in opposite directions.

WOF
Width of fabric.

WOFQ
Width of fat quarter.

2½in strips
Precut strips, often referred to as "Jelly Rolls" or "Rolie Polie," which are 2½in (6.4cm) wide and 20–22in (51–56cm) long.

Index

A
advanced level
  High Fidelity 122–7
  Light My Fire 106–13
  Quilt 54 100–5
  Retro Blooms 114–21
  Trippy Dippy 94–9
appliqué 24–5
Appliqué Adventure
  (intermediate) 86–93
  templates 136–9
assembling, quilt 14–17
Aurifil thread 10, 16

B
backings, pillow 26–7
basting 14
bed runner appliqué 93
beginner level
  Chevy 32–7
  Good Vibes 44–9
  Static 38–43
  Stevie Pillow 50–5
binding 16–7
blades
  pointed 22
  wedge 23

C
Checkered Adventure
  (intermediate) 74–9
  templates 136–9
Chevy (beginner) 32–7
concave curve 18, 21
confident beginner level
  Flower Power 68–73
  Outta Sight 62–7
  Patio Lanterns 56–61
convex curve 18, 21
corners, adding 28
curves 18–19, 21
cutting mat, self-healing 10

D
Dresden plate units 22–3
Drunkard's Path unit 18–20

E
edging 17
envelope pillow back 26

F
fabric 12–13
fabric prep 14
finishing ideas 17
Flower Power (confident
  beginner) 68–73
  templates 133
fusibles 12, 25

G
glue 12, 19
Good Vibes (beginner) 44–9

H
half circle curves 21
Half circle units 21
hand quilting 16
hand stitching 17
hanging, wall 28–9
  appliqué 92
High Fidelity (advanced)
  122–7
  templates 134–5

I
intermediate level
  Appliqué Adventure 86–93
  Checkered Adventure 74–9
  Op Art 80–5
iron/ironing board 10

L
labeling 13
large quilts 14

Light My Fire (advanced)
  106–13

M
marker, water soluble 12, 16
masking tape 16, 20
mat, self-healing cutting 10
materials/tools 10–13

N
nothing for curves, using 19, 21

O
Op Art (intermediate) 80–5
Outta Sight (confident
  beginner) 62–7
  templates 135

P
Patio Lanterns (confident
  beginner) 56–61
  templates 133
pillow appliqué 90
pillow backings 26–7
  envelope 26
  round/shaped 27
pillow insert 27
pins 12, 18, 21
placemat appliqué 90–1
presser foot 10

Q
Quilt 54 (advanced) 100–5
quilt assembling 14–17
quilting 16

R
raw edge appliqué 12, 24
Retro Blooms (advanced)
  114–21
  templates 128–9
ripper, seam 10

rotary cutter 10
round/shaped pillow back 27
rulers, quilting 10

S

scissors, fabric 12
seam ripper 10
self-healing cutting mat 10
sewing machine 10
skill levels 13
   advanced 94–127
   beginner 32–55
   confident beginner 56–73
   intermediate 74–93
snowball corner 118
starch 12
Static (beginner) 38–43
Stevie Pillow (beginner) 50–5
   templates 129–31

T

table/bed runner appliqué 93
techniques
   appliqué 24–5
   Dresden plate units 22–3
   Drunkard's Path unit 18–20
   Half circle units 21
   pillow backings 26–7
   wall hanging 28–9
templates 12, 128–39
   Appliqué Adventure 136–9
   Checkered Adventure 136–9
   Flower Power 133
   High Fidelity 134–5
   Outta Sight 135
   Patio Lanterns 133
   Retro Blooms 128–9
   Stevie Pillow 129–31
   Trippy Dippy 132
thread 10, 16
tools/materials 10–13

trims, different 17, 20, 92
Trippy Dippy (advanced) 94–9
  templates 132
turned edge fusible appliqué 12, 25
tweezers/stiletto, sewing 12

W

wall hanging 28–9
 appliqué 92
water soluble marker 12, 16

Acknowledgments

This book would not have happened without the support of many, so I would like to offer my gratitude and thanks to them all.

First, to my husband Morgan, and our kids Charlie and Benny. Thank you for all your support, and for helping out with life while I was buried under fabric or stationed at my computer. You've helped me make another dream come true. You are all amazing, and I love you with all my heart!

To my parents, Mark, Martha, and Sandy, as well as my in-laws, Becky and Richard, I appreciate you all. To my Grandma Marion, thank you for always shining your love down on me.

My Sew Sister, Belle Brunner: I love you. Radha Weaver, Shannon Boyer, Caitlin Theobald, Natalie Rosesky, Katy Brown, Carli Marsico, Katherine and Chase, and Steve McGuire: Thank you for your support, it's meant a lot! Jan Ditchfield and Elizabeth Chappell, thank you for always being there, and being my mentors. I appreciate you!

Kim Forman, I could not have done this book without you! You took the time to teach me and you kept me sane throughout this process. You are the best tech editor and I'm so glad to call you my friend.

Thank you so much to Meagan, Melody, and the Ruby Star Society team, as well as the team at Moda Fabrics. You have all been incredibly generous and supportive! (Readers, please check them out at rubystarsociety.com and modafabrics.com!)

Sylvia of Honeybee Quilt Studio, you made these quilts sing with your longarming. Thank you so much for being a part of this project, your vision and expertise amazes me. I appreciate you, friend! (Find Sylvia at honeybeequiltstudio.ca!)

And finally, to you! Thank you so much for picking up this book. I hope you've enjoyed making these retro quilts. Please tag me on social media @theretroquilter— I always love to see your makes. Keep creative and stay cool!

A DAVID AND CHARLES BOOK
© Quarto Publishing plc 2025

David and Charles is an imprint of David and Charles, Ltd
Suite A, Tourism House, Pynes Hill, Exeter, EX2 5WS

Conceived, edited, and designed by Quarto Publishing, an imprint of
The Quarto Group, 1 Triptych Place, London, SE1 9SH

First published in the UK and USA in 2025

Maude MacDonald has asserted her right to be identified as author of this
work in accordance with the Copyright, Designs and Patents Act, 1988.

All rights reserved. No part of this publication may be reproduced in any form
or by any means, electronic or mechanical, by photocopying, recording or
otherwise, without prior permission in writing from the publisher.

The author and publisher have made every effort to ensure that all the
instructions in the book are accurate and safe, and therefore cannot accept
liability for any resulting injury, damage or loss to persons or property,
however it may arise.

Names of manufacturers and product ranges are provided for the information
of readers, with no intention to infringe copyright or trademarks.

A catalogue record for this book is available from the British Library.

ISBN-13: 9781446315903 paperback
ISBN-13: 9781446315927 EPUB

This book has been printed on paper from approved suppliers and made from
pulp from sustainable sources.

Printed in China.

10 9 8 7 6 5 4 3 2 1

Commissioning editor: Lily de Gatacre
Assistant editor: Ella Whiting
Copy editor: Marie Clayton
Technical editor: Kim Forman
Designer: Hello Daly
Art director: Martina Calvio
Photographer: Leanne Jade
Stylist: Claire Montgomerie
Production manager: David Hearn
Managing editor: Emma Harverson
Publisher: Lorraine Dickey

Printable versions of the templates are available to download free from
www.bookmarkedhub.com. Search for this book by the title or ISBN: the
files can be found under 'Book Extras'. Membership of the Bookmarked
online community is free.

David and Charles publishes high-quality books on a wide range of subjects.
For more information visit www.davidandcharles.com.

Follow us on Instagram by searching for @dandcbooks.

Layout of the digital edition of this book may vary depending on reader
hardware and display settings.

MIX
Paper | Supporting
responsible forestry
FSC® C016973